ASIAN AMERICAN CHRONOLOGY

ASIAN AMERICAN CHRONOLOGY

**Edited by Deborah G. Baron
and Susan B. Gall**

*An imprint of Gale Research,
An ITP Information/Reference Group Company*

I(T)P

Changing the Way the World Learns

NEW YORK • LONDON • BONN • BOSTON • DETROIT
MADRID • MELBOURNE • MEXICO CITY • PARIS
SINGAPORE • TOKYO • TORONTO • WASHINGTON
ALBANY NY • BELMONT CA • CINCINNATI OH

ASIAN AMERICAN CHRONOLOGY

Deborah G. Baron and Susan B. Gall, *Editors*

Staff

Sonia Benson, *U•X•L Developmental Editor*
Carol DeKane Nagel, *U•X•L Managing Editor*
Thomas L. Romig, *U•X•L Publisher*

Shanna Heilveil, *Production Associate*
Evi Seoud, *Assistant Production Manager*
Mary Beth Trimper, *Production Director*

Michelle DiMercurio, *Art Director*
Cynthia Baldwin, *Product Design Manager*

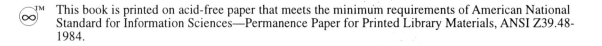 ∞™ This book is printed on acid-free paper that meets the minimum requirements of American National Standard for Information Sciences—Permanence Paper for Printed Library Materials, ANSI Z39.48-1984.

ISBN 0-8103-9692-0
Printed in the United States of America

10 9 8 7 6 5 4 3 2 1

I(T)P™ U•X•L is an imprint of Gale Research,
an International Thomson Publishing Companhy
ITP logo is a trademark under license.

CONTENTS

READER'S GUIDE

Asian American Chronology explores significant social, political, economic, cultural, and professional milestones in Asian American history. Arranged by year and then by month and day where applicable, the chronology spans from prehistory to modern times. Entries range from a few lines to one page in length and describe topics such as immigration, discriminatory legislation, the world wars, the formation of activist organizations, and the contributions Asian Americans have made to all aspects of American society. The *Chronology* contains more than 90 illustrations and maps as well as charts and boxes that highlight important information. The extensively cross-referenced volume concludes with a list of sources for further reading or research and a cumulative subject index.

Related Reference Sources:

Asian American Biography profiles more than 130 Americans who trace their ancestry to Asia and the Pacific Islands. Included are prominent men and women of Asian Indian, Cambodian, Chinese, Filipino, Native Hawaiian, Hmong, Japanese, Pacific Island, Pakistani, Taiwanese, and Vietnamese descent, both living and deceased. Profilees are notable for their achievements in fields ranging from civil rights to sports, politics to academia, entertainment to science, religion to the military. Early leaders in Asian American as well as contemporary figures are among those included. A black-and-white photograph accompanies most entries, and a list of sources for further reading or research is provided at the end of each entry. Cross-references to other profiles in these volumes are noted in bold letters within the text. The volumes are arranged alphabetically and conclude with an index listing all individuals by field of endeavor.

Asian American Almanac explores the history and culture of the major ethnic groups comprising Asian America. The *Almanac* is organized into 15 subject chapters, including immigration patterns, women and family, religion, employment, civil rights and activism, education, literature and theater, and sports. The volume contains more than 70 black-and-white photographs and maps, a glossary, and a cumulative subject index.

Asian American Voices presents full or excerpted speeches, sermons, orations, poems, testimony, and other notable spoken works of Asian Americans. Each entry is accompanied by an introduction and boxes explaining some of the terms and events to which the speech refers. The volume is illustrated with black-and-white photographs and drawings and features a cumulative subject index.

Comments and Suggestions

We welcome your comments on Asian American Biography as well as your suggestions for persons to be featured in future editions. Please write: Editors, Asian American Biography, U•X•L, 835 Penobscot Bldg., Detroit, Michigan 48226-4094; call toll-free: 1-800-877-4253; or fax: 1-313-961-6348.

Advisors

Special thanks are due for the invaluable comments and suggestions provided by U•X•L's Asian American advisors:

Patricia Baird and Patricia Fagel,
    Librarians, Media Resource Center
    Shaker Heights Middle School,
    Shaker Heights, Ohio
Jeanne Dubose Goka,
    Curriculum Director
    St. Michael's Academy
    Austin, Texas
Lin Look
    Librarian, Tenley Friendship Branch
    District of Columbia Public Library
James W. Miller, Teacher
    Woodrow Wilson Middle School
    Newton, Massachusetts

PHOTO CREDITS

The photographs and illustrations appearing in *Asian American Chronology* were received from the following sources:

Cover: Chinese immigrants as they arrive aboard the *Shinyu Maru*: **UPI/Bettmann.**

U.S. Bureau of Census: page 5; **Maryland Cartographics:** page 6; **Library of Congress:** pages 9 ,13 14, 142; **Yale University Archives:** page 10; **Burlington Northern Railroad:** page 12; **Bancroft Library:** page 16; **Office of Hawaiian Affairs:** page 17; **Connie Young Yu:** pages 18, 19; **Photograph by Floyd Lumbard, courtesy of Lee and Barbara Lumbard:** page 21; **U.S. Army Military History Institute:** pages 24, 70, 93; **Corel Corporation:** page 25; **AP/Wide World:** page 28, 31, 45, 87, 89, 91, 94, 95, 104, 106, 114, 115, 120, 127, 131, 141, 144, 146, 151; ; **Jon Melegrito:** page 30, 35; **Morikami Museum:** pages 32, 50, 110; **U.S. Military Academy Archives:** page 33; **Courtesy of the Academy of Motion Picture Arts and Sciences:** page 37; **Photograph by Hope Cahill, courtesy of Connie Young Yu:** page 41; **International Swimming Hall of Fame:** pages 42, 86, 131; **Courtesy of Daniel K. Inouye:** pages 52, 97; **E.P. Dutton & Co., Inc.:** page 54; **Courtesy of Norman Mineta:** pages 57, 134; **Photograph by Christian Steiner, courtesy of Seiji Ozawa:** page 59; **Photography by Christian Steiner, courtesy of Sony Classical:** page 60; Adapted from **National Archives:** page 67; **U.S. Army Center of Military History:** page 71; **Courtesy of Ping Chong:** page 73; **Bancroft Library:** page 78; **U.S. Army Signal Corps:** page 80; **National Aeronautics and Space Administration (NASA):** page 82; **Photo by Tony Esparza, courtesy of CBS Inc.:** page 84; **Courtesy of Dale Minami:** page 85; **Courtesy of Hiram Fong:** page 96; **Photograph by Minoru Yamasaki:** page 98; **Photograph by Frank Wolfe, courtesy of LBJ Library Collection:** page 100; **Photography by Yoichi R. Okamoto, courtesy of LBJ Library Collection:** page 103; **Courtesy of Harry Kitano:** page 105; **Courtesy of Robert Matsui:** page 107; **Courtesy of Huynh Cong Ut:** page 108; **Photograph by Susan Gilbert, courtesy of Jeanne Wakatsuki Houston:** page 109; **Photograph by Harry Langdon Photography, courtesy of March Fong Eu:** page 111; **Courtesy of Senator Daniel Akaka:** page 112; **Courtesy of Thomas Tang:** page 116; **Photograph by Bjorn Elgstrand, courtesy of Subrahmanyan Chandrasekhar:** page 122; **Photograph by Ingbet Grüttner, courtesy of Pei Cobb Freed & Partners:** page 123; **Courtesy of S. B. Woo:** page 126; **Courtesy of Haing S. Ngor:** page 128; **Courtesy of Houghton Mifflin:** pages 135, 143; **Photograph by Russ Adams Productions, courtesy of ATP Tour:** page 136; **Courtesy of ICM Artists, Ltd.:** page 137; **Courtesy of Christine Choy:** page 138; **Courtesy of G. P. Putnam's Sons:** page 139; **Courtesy of Steven**

Asian Americans: Who Are They?

Asian Americans are identified in many different ways, but they all have one thing in common—their ancestors came from one of over 20 Asian nations. An Asian American's ancestors could have left any of these countries to make their home in the United States: Bangladesh, Bhutan, Cambodia (including Hmong), China (including Hong Kong or Taiwan), India, Indonesia, Japan, Korea, Laos, Malaysia, Mongolia, Myanmar (Burma), Nepal, Pakistan, the Philippines, Singapore, Sri Lanka, Thailand, and Vietnam. Sometimes the term Asian American is expanded to Asian Pacific American, to include natives of the Pacific Islands, especially Hawaii, American Samoa, and Guam. Individual groups may be referred to by their country of origin—such as Chinese American or Filipino American (from the Philippines). Asian Americans together represent the fastest growing segment of the U.S. population. Statisticians predict that Asian Americans, about 3 percent of the population in 1990, will grow to represent about 12 percent by the year 2000. ☉

11,000 B.C.

Small groups of Asian hunters crossed the Bering Sea Land Bridge (now under the waters of the Bering Strait) from Asia to Alaska.

800 B.C.

Evidence of Asian influence appeared in pottery of Native Americans in Alaska.

A.D. 300–750

Seafaring Polynesians, probably from Southeast Asia, settled the South Pacific Islands, particularly the remote northern islands we now know as Hawaii. They brought with them the important elements of their culture, including the staple foods of their diet: taro (a starchy root plant), coconuts, and bananas.

900–1000

Filipino natives, who had descended from Malaysian stock and who had been rice farming and fishing in the Philippine Islands for about 30,000 years, extended their trade activities from Malaysia to China.

1565–1815

Filipinos, under Spanish rule since Portugese navigator Ferdinand Magellan claimed the islands for Spain in 1521, were forced to serve in the Manila

Galleon Trade between the Philippines and Mexico. (Galleons were large Spanish ships used for trading and warfare.) Asian goods were shipped to Manila in the Philippines by galleon, and from there to Acapulco, Mexico, en route to Spain.

These Filipinos are thought to be the earliest Asians to cross the Pacific Ocean in transit to North America.

1587   **October 18.** The Spanish galleon *Nuestra Señora de Esperanza* (Our Lady of Hope) landed in present-day California, the first recorded incident of Filipinos arriving in what is now the the continental United States. The Filipino crew members served as scouts for the landing party of explorers on the ship.

1763   Filipinos serving in the Manila Galleon Trade between the Philippines and Mexico settled in present-day Louisiana after jumping ship to escape the brutality of their Spanish officers. *(Also see entry dated 1565–1815.)*

They settled along the Mississippi River Delta, building their villages on stilts and fishing and hunting for their livelihood.

1778   Captain James Cook, an English navigator, first charted the Hawaiian islands, naming them the Sandwich Islands after his patron, John Montagu, fourth earl of Sandwich. Each of the islands was ruled by a chief under a hereditary system called *kapu.* When Cook arrived, these rulers were at war with one another. Kamehameha was the powerful chief of the largest island, Hawaii. *(Also see entry dated 1810.)*

1781   Pueblo de Nuestra Señora Reina de los Angeles, now the city of Los Angeles, California, was founded. One of the 46 founders was Antonio Miranda, of Philippine ancestry. California at that time was a Spanish settlement.

1785   Three Chinese crewmen—Asing, Achyun, and Accun—from a U.S. cargo ship were stranded in Baltimore, Maryland, for almost a year. At that time, contact between the American colonies and China was limited to trade between the two. The three crewmen lived on public funds in the care of Levi Hollingsworth, a merchant, until they could return to China.

1787   **September 17.** The U.S. Constitution was signed at the Pennsylvania State House in Philadelphia, presently Independence Hall. Over the following months, each of the thirteen colonies held elections to ratify, or formally approve, the new document.

1788   **June 21.** New Hampshire ratified the U.S. Constitution. In order for the Constitution to become law, two-thirds, or nine of the thirteen original colonies, had to ratify it. New Hampshire was the ninth colony to formally approve the document. The new constitutional government would go into effect in March 1789.

1790   The first U.S. Naturalization Act allowed only "free white persons" to become American citizens.

Naturalization is the process by which the rights of citizenship of a particular country are granted to those who were not born there but chose to settle there.

The first Asian Indian arrived in Salem, Massachusetts, from Madras, India, on a British trading vessel.

1791   **December 15.** The Bill of Rights (the first ten amendments to the U.S. Constitution) was ratified and became part of the Constitution. These amendments guaranteed certain rights: freedom of religion, freedom of speech, freedom of assembly, freedom to bear arms, freedom from unreasonable searches, and the right to a fair and speedy trial by an impartial jury.

1802   A Chinese "sugar master" reportedly arrived in Hawaii on a trading ship, bringing boiling pans and other sugar-making paraphernalia. By the 1830s, several Chinese sugar mills were in operation on the islands of Maui and Hawaii. (*Also see entry dated 1835.*)

1806   Eight shipwrecked Japanese sailors were picked up by an American ship and taken to Honolulu, Hawaii. (The Tokugawa Shogunate [government] in Japan had a strict isolationist policy prohibiting Japanese from leaving or returning to Japan, upon penalty of death. Isolationism is a national policy of avoiding entanglement in foreign affairs; in this case, it served to effectively cut Japan off from the rest of the world.) The eight sailors became the first Japanese to arrive in the Kingdom of Hawaii.

1810 After many years of wars between the chiefs of the Hawaiian islands, Kamehameha I, the powerful ruler of the island of Hawaii, declared himself head of a royal dynasty of the Kingdom of Hawaii. Kamehameha's dynasty brought peace to the islands, and the new king promoted agriculture and trade with Americans and Chinese. However, European and American traders brought devastating diseases to the native population, killing many. Traders also brought alcohol, firearms, and European or Western customs, which weakened the native culture and religious traditions.

1815 Filipino settlers in Louisiana fought with French pirate Jean Laffitte against the British during the Battle of New Orleans (fought after the War of 1812 had ended—American military leader Andrew Jackson had not heard that peace had been made with the British). Victory in this battle ultimately led to the American acquisition of Louisiana as a state.

1820 Under the reign of Kamehameha III, Protestant missionaries arrived in Hawaii. Reverend Hiram Bingham, a pastor based in Honolulu, was a leader in bringing Christianity to the Hawaiian Islands. Missionaries established schools and developed a Hawaiian alphabet so the Bible could be translated.

1830 For the first time, the U.S. census noted the number of Chinese in America—the count was three. There were certainly more Chinese in the United States at that time, but the census questionnaire did not include a question about race or ethnicity—the census-taker must have added the information voluntarily. For the next two decades, racial information was not specifically requested on the census questionnaire. In 1840, Chinese numbered eight, but by 1850 the figure was 758. In 1870, a category for Chinese was added to the census form. Nonetheless, until 1870, census figures neglected significant numbers of Asians and Pacific Islanders in the United States.

1833 Filipinos settled in the fishing village of St. Malo at the mouth of the Mississippi River. The village would be completely destroyed by a hurricane 60 years later.

1835 The first American sugar plantation was established in Hawaii. (*Also see entry dated 1802.*)

1839 Kamehameha III created a constitutional monarchy in Hawaii. Three years later an American, G. P. Judd, became the prime minister of Hawaii and held the post until 1854. Commercial ties between the United States and Hawaii grew, particularly as American business executives became interested in Hawaii's prosperous sugar industry.

THE GREAT TRIBULATION.

Cartoon of a census-taker in 1860

1839–42 The Opium War was fought between England and China over the importation of opium from India—then a colony of England—into China. Opium is a highly addictive narcotic drug that the Chinese wanted to outlaw. England forcefully defeated China. The turning point in the conflict came when the English retaliated after the Chinese burned an English ship loaded with opium.

China, which had isolated itself since 221 B.C. with the building of the fortified Great Wall, did not open the port of Guangzhou (Canton) to international trade until 1757. And until 1842, Guangzhou was the only Chinese port open. Emporer Chi'en Lung, of China's ruling Manchu dynasty (a powerful group or family), was responsible for the opening of Guangzhou to foreign commerce. Until that time China had pursued a strict policy of isolationism, in which it virtually cut itself off from the rest of the world. The dynastic rulers forbade emigration on pain of death. They believed that China alone embodied civilization. Other peoples, particularly those from the West (Europe and North America), were viewed as uncultured and barbaric. The Manchus also feared Western influence, believing that competition resulting from foreign trade would adversely affect the delicate Chinese economy. Such destabilization of the economy, coupled with Western political philosophies, posed a grave threat to the rulers of China, who believed that isolationism would protect their power. When the Chinese lost the Opium War, they were forced to open more ports to foreign trade and to give up certain territories, among them Hong Kong, which was ceded to Britain.

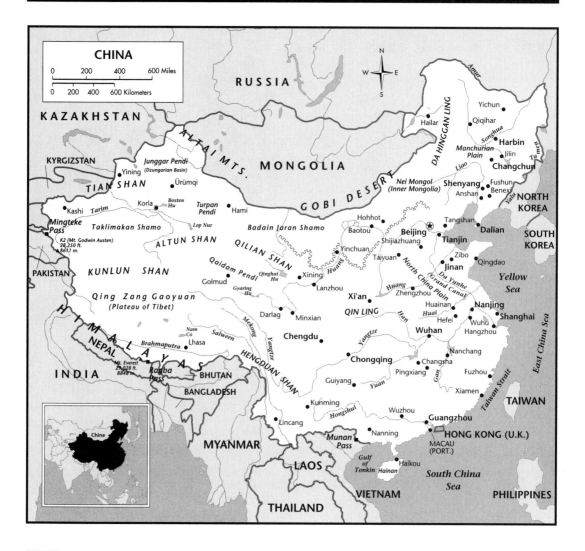

1840   Hawaii adopted its first written constitution, providing for a legislature and a supreme court. The legislature had two houses: a council of chiefs and an elected house of representatives.

1842   The United States recognized the Kingdom of Hawaii as an independent government. (*Also see entries dated 1778 and 1839.*)

1843   **May 7.** The first Japanese arrived in the United States. The best known of these was Manjiro Nakahama, also known as John Mung. He was rescued at sea by

Romanization of Chinese characters

The written Chinese language has no alphabet. About 50,000 characters are used to communicate in print in Chinese. A person must learn about 5,000 characters to read a Chinese newspaper or novel. To write a Chinese word in the Roman alphabet (the 26 letters used in written English), a system of *romanization* is used. In the late 1800s, two British diplomats, Thomas Wade and Herbert Giles, developed a system of romanization for Chinese that was used for several decades. When the Chinese Communist Party won control of the government in 1949, they introduced many new policies and standards. One of the changes the Communists made was to establish *pinyin*, a standard system of writing Chinese using the Roman alphabet. Thirty years later, in 1979, the government of China was using only pinyin in official communications and news reports, having replaced the Wade-Giles system completely. Many proper names were changed. (For example, the port city of Canton became Guangzhou; the name of the man who led the Communist Revolution in 1949, Mao Tse-tung, became Mao Zedong.) ☼

an American whaling ship and subsequently educated at Fairhaven, Massachusetts. In 1860, he served as interpreter for the first official Japanese delegation to visit the United States. John Mung died in Japan in 1898.

1846　Two men from Manila, the Philippines, applied for Hawaiian citizenship in Honolulu during the reign of King Kalakaua.

1848　Chinese began to arrive in the United States, some as indentured servants (immigrants bound by contract to service in a foreign country), during the California Gold Rush. (On January 24, 1848, gold was discovered on the American River, in north central California; people flocked to the state to search for gold. Within seven years, the population of California had grown from 15,000 to a whopping 300,000.) The bulk of these Chinese immigrants later became a source of cheap labor for railroads, mines, fisheries, farms, orchards, canneries, garment and cigar factories, and bootmakers. (*Also see entry dated 1852.*)

Hawaii provided for ownership of private property. Until 1848, all land was owned by the Hawaiian chiefs. But King Kamehameha III and the other chiefs gave most of their land to the Hawaiian government, and the Hawaiian people were allowed to buy or claim parcels of it. This land reform, called the Great Mahele, also allowed for rapid expansion of sugar plantations.

1850   A Japanese man, Hikozo Hamada, also known as Joseph Heco, was rescued at sea by an American sailing ship. He studied in Baltimore, Maryland, and became the first Japanese naturalized as an American citizen.

California, in order to limit the income of foreign gold prospectors, initiated a Foreign Miners' Tax. It was enforced mainly among the Chinese, though it had been designed to apply to all foreigners.

July 23. Groups of Chinese were honored by being invited to march in President Zachary Taylor's "grand funeral pageant" in New York.

1851   The Chinese people rebelled against Western exploitation of China in the T'ai P'ing Rebellion. The revolt was crushed in 1864, leaving widespread devastation, famine, and inflation. At the time, China was beset by internal political disorder and economic uncertainty. The problems were attributed to the presence of Westerners, who had in fact come to China to exploit new markets and resources. The ruling Manchus blamed all of China's ills on the West (though they themselves were responsible for much of the turmoil).

In 1851 an uprising against the Manchus was instigated by rural peasants who could no longer stand the economic hardship facing them. Originating in the southern province of Kwangsi, the revolt broadened into a widespread conflict.

In an odd twist of events, the West was called on by the Manchus to help crush the T'ai P'ing Rebellion. In the end, 30 million lives were lost, large farming districts were destroyed, and the Manchu government was severely weakened, which led to even greater Western control of China.

1852   More than 20,000 Chinese, desperately seeking a new life after the start of the T'ai P'ing uprising in China in 1851 (see entry above), poured into San Francisco, California, on their way to the gold fields of the Sierra Nevada Mountains. They called the United States *Gum San*, which means "the gold mountain."

These early arrivals were almost all men (which resulted in so-called bachelor societies), since respectable Chinese women could not leave their parents' or in-laws' homes. The population of Chinese men in San Francisco encouraged the growth of Chinese-owned businesses, such as groceries and firms that imported Chinese textiles and clothing. *(Also see entries dated 1848 and 1851.)*

Groups of Chinese marched at President Zachary Taylor's funeral procession, 1850

1853   Partly due to the Foreign Miners' Tax imposed by California, Chinese immigration was reduced to 5,000 from the approximately 20,000 that had entered the state the year before. Many Chinese headed for Australia after the news of gold discovery there.

1854   The Chinese Six Companies were organized to protect and regulate Chinese communities.

Formed by merchants in the Chinese community in response to widespread murderous attacks on the Chinese in California, the Chinese Six Companies became advocates for the community, negotiating with the government and hiring attorneys to fight unjust laws.

9

Yung Wing became the first Chinese American to graduate from a U.S. college, Yale University.

Wing later returned to China and sought permission to recruit 120 boys for an education mission in Connecticut and Massachusetts. The mission was withdrawn several years later due to alarm on the part of the Chinese Imperial Court that the boys were being subjected to harmful Western influences. *(Also see entry dated 1839–42.)*

Yung Wing

In *Hall* v. *People*, the California Supreme Court reversed the conviction of George Hall for murdering a Chinese man on the grounds that the decision had been based on the testimony of Chinese witnesses. The Criminal Act of 1850 provided that "No Black or Mulatto person, or Indian, shall be allowed to give evidence in favor of, or against a White Man."

The chief justice ruled that the Criminal Act actually included "Asiatics" who had crossed the Bering Strait into Alaska. Testimony from Chinese was almost never accepted after this time except in cases involving other Chinese. *(Also see entry dated 11,000 B.C.)*

1856 Foreign miners were harshly taxed to prevent Chinese from panning for gold. This was one example of the growing anti-Chinese feeling, fueled by fear that the Chinese "stole" jobs because they were willing to work for low wages. *(Also see entries dated 1850 and 1853.)*

1859 Chinese were excluded from public schools in San Francisco by order of the California Superintendent of Education. He allowed state funds to be withheld from schools that admitted Chinese, and eventually the California legislature mandated separate schools for them.

1860   The first official Japanese delegation visited the United States; Manjiro Naka-hama served as interpreter. *(Also see entry dated 1843.)*

Between December 1860 and February 1861, seven southern states—Alabama, Georgia, Florida, Louisiana, Mississippi, South Carolina, and Texas—withdrew from the United States and formed a separate government, known as the Confederate States of America, or the Confederacy, with Jefferson Davis as president.

1861   **April 12.** The Confederacy launched a battle at Fort Sumter in the harbor of Charleston, South Carolina, which marked the beginning of the U.S. Civil War. Arkansas, North Carolina, Virginia, and Tennessee joined the Confederacy in response to the outbreak of war. An estimated 360,000 Union (U.S. government) soldiers would die of various causes over the next four years, including 110,000 killed in battle. Confederate losses were estimated to be 250,000, with 94,000 killed in battle.

1862   Congress enacted a law that allowed "any alien" honorably discharged from U.S. military service to apply for naturalization. *(Also see entry dated 1790.)*

The Joint Select Committee Relative to the Chinese Population of the State of California found that the Chinese contributed $14,000,000 to the state's economy and declared in its report, "They work for us, they help build up our State by contributing largely to our taxes, to our shopping, farming, and mechanical interests, without to any extent entering these departments as competitors...."

1863   Recruiting began for Chinese laborers for the Central Pacific Railroad.

In all, 10,000 to 12,000 Chinese workers laid track and carved ledges and tunnels for this branch of the Transcontinental Railroad between 1865 and 1869. Approximately 1,200 were killed by explosives or by avalanches during the brutal winters of the Sierra Nevada mountains.

1864   **November 28.** Supposed birthdate of Philip Jaisohn, the first Korean to become an American citizen and first Korean American to receive an American medical degree.

Chinese labor on the Northern Pacific Railway in the 1880s

Jaisohn was born Suh Jae-pil in the South Cholla Province of Korea, the son of parents who were members of the most privileged social class in Korea. He used an Anglicized version of his name upon his arrival in the United States in 1885, becoming Philip Jaisohn. He received his medical degree in 1892 and four years later returned to Korea to establish the first Korean newspaper. There, he became involved in the fight to keep Korea independent of China and, after 1910, to liberate it from Japan. Jaisohn devoted the majority of his life to the cause of Korean independence. His work in medical research and pathology (the study of diseases) and for Korean causes gained respect in both his homeland and his adopted country, the United States. Jaisohn died in 1951.

1867   About 40,000 Chinese arrived in the United States from 1867 to 1870, partly due to recruitment by the Central Pacific Railroad. *(Also see entry dated 1863.)*

A meeting of the Workingmen's Party in California

1868   The first Japanese were recruited and transported from Japan by American, German, and Dutch interests to work in Hawaii, Guam, and California—even though labor emigration was still illegal in Japan. About 149 Japanese contract workers arrived in Hawaii to work the sugar plantations. But they were so poorly treated that the Japanese government brought at least 40 of them home.

The United States ratified the Burlingame Treaty with China, which recognized the right of Chinese to immigrate for "purpose of curiosity, trade, or permanent residence," but which expressly restricted the right of naturalization.

1869   The Knights of Labor, an American labor organization, was formed in this year by Philadelphia tailors to counteract the growing power of big business, particularly in heavy manufacturing. The Knights of Labor and the Workingmen's Party would actively oppose immigration, making immigrant workers scapegoats for labor problems. The Knights of Labor engaged in many labor strikes, often resorting to violent confrontation.

European and Asian workers completing the last mile of the Central Pacific Railroad

Wakamatsu Tea and Silk Colony was established by a group of Japanese exiles at Gold Hill (Coloma), California. They were the first Japanese to immigrate to the continental United States after the fall of the isolationist Tokugawa government and the return of imperial rule in Japan. (Imperial rule is that of an emperor or empire.) The grave of "Okei," one of the members of the colony, commemorates the site.

May 10. The Transcontinental Railroad, part of the extensive economic expansion after the end of the Civil War, was completed. Spikes of Nevada silver and California gold were driven into a railroad tie made of wood from a California laurel tree to join the western and eastern railroad lines at Promontory, Utah. The hammer that drove in the spike was connected to telegraph wires so that the sound would be carried across the country. The western line, the Central

U.S. Census: Asian and Pacific Islander Categories, 1790–1990

Here is the history of the categories used by the U.S. Census Bureau when collecting information about the people of the United States. Every ten years, the Census Bureau gathers detailed information about about the population of the United States. This is called the Decennial Census. ✺

Year of the Decennial Census	Asian of Pacific Islander Category
1790	First census includes only the categories of white, slaves, and other.
1870	Chinese category added.
1890	Japanese category added.
1950	Filipino category added.
1960	Hawaiian and Part Hawaiian categories added.
1970	Hawaiian and Part Hawaiian categories combined into a single category, Hawaiian/Part Hawaiian.
1980	Asian Indian, Vietnamese categories added; Guamanian and Samoan added.
1990	Other A/PI [Asian/Pacific Islander] (specify) _____. added.

Source: U.S. Bureau of Census, Decennial Censuses of Population

Pacific Railroad, originated in Sacramento, California; the eastern line, the Union Pacific, stemmed from Omaha, Nebraska. The Golden Spike National Historic Site of the connection at Promontory Point, Utah, commemorates the site of the connection and the event. Ninety percent of the laborers who built the Central Pacific Railroad through the Sierra Nevada mountains were Chinese immigrants.

1870   The Naturalization Act of 1870 excluded Chinese from citizenship and prohibited the entry into the United States of wives of Chinese laborers. Asian population in the United States exceeded 105,000.

A nationwide recession resulted in a decrease in jobs available to West Coast laborers. "Cheap Chinese labor" once again became the scapegoat. Mobs destroyed Chinese communities in many areas of California and other states.

15

In San Francisco, the Board of Supervisors imposed fees on laundry delivery wagons according to the number of horses used. The highest fees were reserved for laundries that used no horses—Chinese laundries.

1871 In Los Angeles's Chinatown, violence erupted when a crowd gathered to witness a fight over a woman between two Chinese factions. Non-Chinese men in the crowd began firing at the Chinese who were running for the safety of their homes. By the time the riot was subdued, fifteen Chinese had been hanged by the mob, four had been shot, and two were wounded.

Mobs destroy buildings in Chinatown

Immigration records from 1871 through 1899 show a total of 491 Asian Indian entrants to the United States.

1873 Zun Zow Matzmulla became the first Japanese midshipman to attend the U.S. Naval Academy, graduating in 1873.

1874 In Hawaii, King Kalakaua, known as the Merry Monarch, ascended to the throne. He reinstated many Hawaiian traditions that had been banned by Christian missionaries, such as the hula (a rhythmic dance marked by the swaying of the hips). Hawaiian music and the custom of wearing grass skirts, brought to Hawaii by laborers from Samoa, grew in popularity.

1875 Seth Lewelling, a farmer in California, developed a new type of cherry with the help of a Chinese employee named Ah Bing. Lewelling named the sweet new fruit the Bing cherry.

The U.S. Congress passed the Page Law, forbidding the entry of Chinese, Japanese, and Mongolian contract laborers, prostitutes, and felons. It was enforced so strictly among prostitutes that all women had to undergo a rigorous examination by U.S. officials in China before being allowed to emigrate. This was so intimidating that even wives of Chinese laborers were discouraged from coming to the United States. When the fiancée of Lee Yoke Suey attempted to join him in California, she was detained by U.S. immigration officials for over 16 months.

1876   In Hawaii, King Kalakaua was struggling through a stormy reign, clashing with the Hawaiian legislature, the powerful sugar plantation owners, and American business people whose interests in the sugar industry comprised a significant political force. A key achievement during his reign was the enactment of the U.S./Hawaii Reciprocity Treaty. This treaty allowed Hawaiian-grown sugar to enter the United States duty-free (without being taxed as an import). The treaty was renewed in 1887, when a clause was added to lease Pearl Harbor to the United States for use as a naval base. *(Also see entries dated 1874 and 1887.)*

Present-day hula dancers in Hawaii

With increasing economic turmoil in the United States, Chinese laborers continued to be viewed as the problem in some communities. Riots and violence directed at Chinese broke out in San Francisco and elsewhere.

1877 Public resentment of the Chinese grew, partly due to widespread unemployment, and groups such as the Knights of Labor and Workingmen's Party cried, "The Chinese Must Go!" Labor group leaders voiced the opinion that the Chinese drove decent white men out of the labor market, causing their families to starve. These groups held labor rallies that often turned into violent demonstrations in which Chinese were attacked. *(Also see entry dated 1869.)*

Wedding photo of Mr. and Mrs. Lee Yoke Suey, around 1900

1880 The U.S. census reported 148 Japanese in the continental United States.

Korea, under Chinese domination since the seventeenth century and so isolated from non-Chinese contact that it was known as the Hermit Kingdom, entered into a commercial treaty with Japan in 1876. Korea then began trade agreements with the United States and several European countries.

November 17. A treaty between the United States and China concluded on this day gave the United States the right to limit immigration of Chinese laborers. The treaty was signed by President Chester A. Arthur on October 5, 1881.

1882 The Chinese Exclusion Act, passed at the insistence of California, prohibited entrance of Chinese laborers and prohibited courts from issuing citizenship to

Chinese under attack

Chinese already in California. This was intended to last for only ten years but was extended twice, first to 1902 and then to last "indefinitely." The Chinese Exclusion Act was not repealed until 1943. *(Also see entries dated 1892, 1902, and December 17, 1943.)*

Chinese workers, particularly launderers and miners, were excessively taxed, and certain occupations were restricted: medicine, teaching, dentistry, mining, railroading, and manufacturing.

Led by Admiral Robert W. Shufeldt, the United States and Korea entered into their first treaty, the United States being only the second nation to strike an accord with Korea. Japan was the first.

Aiiolani Hale ("the House of Heavenly Kings," commonly called the Iolani Palace) in Honolulu served as the official residence of King Kalakaua, Hawaii's last king, until 1891, when Kalakaua's sister, Queen Liliuokalani ascended to the throne. The Iolani Palace was the only royal palace in any location that is today part of the United States. When the monarchy was overthrown in 1893, the palace became the capitol. *(Also see entry dated 1893.)*

1883   The Japanese replaced the Chinese as a source of contract labor in Hawaii. However, the Japanese workers had to sneak out of Japan, as emigration was not made legal there until the following year.

1884   The Japanese government allowed citizens to leave Japan to work as temporary laborers in Hawaii. Until then, emigration from Japan had been illegal, due to the isolationist policy of the Tokugawa Shogunate. *(Also see entry dated 1806.)*

1885   The first 859 legal contract laborers from Japan arrived with their families in the Kingdom of Hawaii following the legalization of emigration in 1884. King Kalakaua was at the dock to welcome them. However, the peaceful existence of the Japanese in Hawaii would prove to be short-lived. *(Also see entry dated December 1906.)*

The Irwin Convention was an agreement negotiated by American Robert Walker Irwin with the Japanese government. Irwin was consul general and special agent of the Board of Immigration of the Kingdom of Hawaii. The Irwin Convention made it illegal for any U.S. citizens to help aliens hired as laborers to immigrate to the United States or its territories. Since most of the ship owners were Americans, the actual goal of the Convention was to stop the flow of Japanese contract laborers to Hawaii. The Convention allowed employment of aliens (notably Japanese) on a temporary basis only.

It is estimated that the pineapple industry was launched in Hawaii in this year. Pineapple plants, shipped to Hawaii from Jamaica under the direction of a British plant expert, provided the first planting for what would become one of Hawaii's major crops by the early 1900s.

The pioneers of the Korean community in the United States were a small group of political and social reformers—expelled from Korea following an unsuccessful attempt to overthrow the government—who arrived as exiles in San Francisco. Among them was Suh Jae-pil, who later adopted the American name Philip Jaisohn. *(Also see entry dated 1864.)*

An "Oriental School" was established by the school board of San Francisco when it denied the right of Chinese children to be educated in public schools. Other segregated schools were opened in California that Chinese children were required to attend until the 1930s. *(Also see entry dated 1859.)*

1887 King Kalakaua renegotiated the U.S./Hawaii Reciprocity Treaty, with many of the same terms as 1868, but giving the United States the right to lease Pearl Harbor and to establish a naval base there. American businessmen had become a dominant power in Hawaii's economics and politics. *(Also see entry dated 1876.)*

Chinese children in California were denied the right to attend public school

1889 In *Chae Chan Ping* v. *U.S.*, the Supreme Court decided that despite the Burlingame Treaty of 1868, the United States could freely prevent Chinese from immigrating to the United States under the Chinese Exclusion Act. *(Also see entries dated 1868 and 1882.)*

1890 Significant Japanese immigration began when laborers, mostly male, relocated to Hawaii. Before 1884, it had been illegal for Japanese to leave or return to Japan. *(Also see entry dated 1884.)*

Most of these emigrants were not seeking a new home but rather the opportunity to make a lot of money and then return to Japan "in glory," using their new wealth to discharge debts, regain lost property, or purchase new land. These workers became known as *sojourners,* settling in Hawaii only temporarily with no plans to assimilate into (adapt to the customs of) Hawaiian society.

Jujiro Wada ("Wadaju") received honorary U.S. citizenship from the governor of the territory of Alaska for his daring rescue of an ice-bound ship by making a long solo journey over ice to Nome, Alaska, for help.

King Kalakaua of Hawaii died during a visit to San Francisco. His sister, Lili-uokalani, became queen. She tried unsuccessfully to gain more power than the constitution of Hawaii provided for its monarch (royal head of state). She would be the last monarch of Hawaii. Her reign lasted less than two years. *(Also see entry dated 1893.)*

August 24. Duke Kahanamoku, native Hawaiian and Olympic swimmer, was born in the palace of Princess Ruth in Honolulu, Hawaii. He was a descendant of early-nineteenth-century Hawaiian King Kamehameha. *(Also see entries dated 1778, August 1911, Summer 1912, 1915, and 1920.)*

1892   The first Japanese-language newspaper in the Kingdom of Hawaii was started in Honolulu.

The Geary Act, an extension of the 1882 Chinese Exclusion Act, prohibited Chinese immigration for another ten years. It also denied Chinese bail and writ of *habeas corpus* (an order requiring that a prisoner receive a hearing by a judge so as to prevent illegal detainment). Under this act, all Chinese in the United States were required to register and carry their registration certificates with them at all times. Any Chinese without a certificate was subject to immediate deportation. *(Also see entry dated 1882.)*

1893   As Hawaii became increasingly controlled by American business interests, Hawaii's Queen Liliuokalani was overthrown in a bloodless revolution after reigning for two years. The overthrow was led by American, German, and British businessmen with backing from American navy and marine forces. Judge Sanford B. Dole, the son of a pioneer missionary to Hawaii, proclaimed the overthrow of the Hawaiian monarchy on the steps of Aliiolani Hale (House of Heavenly Kings) in Honolulu. At this time, John L. Stevens, the U.S. Minister to Hawaii, declared the country a U.S. protectorate. President Grover Cleveland, however, refused to annex Hawaii because he felt that the Americans in the sugar industry had engineered the overthrow of the monarchy, and that the Hawaiian people did not want the revolution. The United States tried to restore Queen Liliuokalani to power, but the provisional (temporary) government would not give up power.

1894 The group that overthrew Queen Liliuokalani formed the Republic of Hawaii and installed Sanford B. Dole as its first president. The U.S. governmment supported a provisional (temporary) government that lasted until Hawaii was annexed as a U.S. territory in 1898. The provisional government was controlled by American business interests, primarily sugar plantation owners. *(Also see entry dated August 12, 1898.)*

1896 In *Yick Wo* v. *Hopkins*, an important civil rights case, the Supreme Court ruled that a San Francisco safety ordinance that was racially neutral but enforced exclusively among Chinese was unconstitutional and a violation of the Fourteenth Amendment. The Fourteenth Amendment promises all people "equal protection of the laws."

When two cases of bubonic plague were discovered in Honolulu's Chinatown, Hawaiian health officials quarantined 4,500 Chinese in a camp and burned Chinatown to the ground. This drastic measure almost certainly reflected the depth of anti-Chinese feelings in Hawaii more than fear of the plague itself.

The first Japanese-language school in the Republic of Hawaii was started by Reverend Takie Okumura at Makiki Christian Church in Honolulu.

José Rizal, leader of the Propaganda Movement in the Philippines, was arrested and executed by the Spanish colonial government for heading an uprising that was actually led by a more radical group.

The Propaganda Movement was organized by the educated *mestizos* (persons of mixed Spanish and American blood) in order to speak out for freedom of speech and representation in the Spanish government of the Philippines and in the Catholic Church.

June 25. The first Hawaii Grand Sumo Tournament was held in Honolulu by Japanese plantation camp workers.

One of the most important sports to the earliest Japanese immigrants, *sumo* is a Japanese form of wrestling where two opponents try to force each other down or outside of a ring in which the action takes place. The sport of sumo was not only a recreational activity to these first immigrants, but something of a symbolic celebration of their heritage. Tournaments held in each plantation camp led to large interisland tournaments such as the Hawaii Grand Sumo Tournament.

The sinking of the USS *Maine* in Havana Harbor

1898   Seven crewmen of Japanese ancestry died in the sinking of the USS *Maine* in Havana Harbor (Cuba). This incident began the Spanish-American War. Other persons of Japanese ancestry served in the U.S. Navy in the Battle of Manila Bay, also part of the Spanish-American War.

The first Japanese-language newspaper in the continental United States, the *Nichi Bei Times* was founded by Abiko Kyutaro (1865–1936) in San Francisco. He later established a Yamato (farming) colony near Livingston, California. (*Also see entries dated 1904 and 1906.*)

August 12. Due to the powerful influence of sugar plantation owners, Hawaii was officially annexed to the United States. President Grover Cleveland, who had opposed annexation and the political domination of Hawaii by American business interests, was succeeded by President William McKinley, who was in favor of annexation. With presidential support, a joint resolution of Congress, approved on July 7, 1898, annexed the Hawaiian Islands. The resolution took effect on August 12.

December 10. The Treaty of Paris, which negotiated the end of the Spanish-American War, ceded the Philippines to the United States.

The Philippines, which had been a Spanish colony for 400 years, strongly resisted American control. Several years of guerrilla warfare followed the surrender of the country to the United States. Filipino nationalists, led by General Emilio Aguinaldo, fought the Americans, culminating in a series of bloody "pacification" battles. An estimated one million Filipinos died as a result of this largely undocumented war.

1899

The North American Buddhist Mission, a forerunner of the Buddhist Churches of America, was incorporated under the laws of California in San Francisco by Japanese missionaries. Their religious services were attended by Japanese and also by European Americans, whose services were conducted in English.

Buddhism, both a religion and philosophy, was founded by Buddha (Siddartha Gautama) in India in the sixth century B.C. It was, and continues to be, an important element in the lives of many Asians and Asian Americans, with over 300 million followers worldwide.

Ahn Chang-ho, a Korean intellectual, arrived in San Francisco to set up residence. In 1903, he established the Chinmok-hoe, or Friendship Society, the first Korean organization in the continental United States. Ten years later he founded the Hung Sa Dang, or Young Koreans Academy, many members of which were active in the Korean National Association. Ahn went

Buddha, "The Enlightened One"

25

The Origin of Buddhism

Buddha, whose given name was Siddhartha Gautama, was born around 563 B.C. in what is today Nepal. At the age of 29, he left his luxurious home to become a wandering monk and seek solutions to the misery of the world. He tried, unsuccessfully, to find enlightenment through yoga masters and through fasting and self-torture for several years. One night, at the age of 35, he sat under a bo (fig) tree in a village in northeast India. In the morning, he awoke with the answers he sought. Thereafter, he became known as the Buddha ("Enlightened One"), and the tree became known as the Bodhi Tree ("Tree of Enlightenment").

Through his enlightenment, Buddha became aware that life is guided by Four Noble Truths. The first is that life is full of sorrow. All living things (people and animals) suffer this sorrow over and over again as they go through a continuous cycle of death and rebirth. The second truth is that this sorrow is brought about by desires and attachment to worldly things. The third truth is that it is possible for people to overcome their desires and the endless cycle of rebirths by reaching *nirvana,* a state of inner peace and happiness. The fourth truth is that nirvana can be attained by living according to the Eightfold Path. To follow this path, people must know the Four Truths, resist doing evil things, say nothing offensive to others, respect life and porperty, work jobs that do not hurt any living thing, have only good thoughts, pay attention to their feelings and bodies, and practice proper concentration. ✪

on to become one of the leaders of the Korean independence movement (Korea was occupied by Japan from 1910 to 1945), serving as secretary of the interior and later as secretary of labor in the provisional government-in-exile set up by expatriate Korean leaders in Shanghai (China) in 1919. He was arrested by Japanese police in 1935 and died shortly after being released from jail three years later. *(Also see entries dated 1903, February 1, 1909, 1913, and 1919.)*

1900   Japanese immigrants began converting California's barren interior into rich vineyards and truck-farming areas. (A truck farm is a farm devoted to growing vegetables for sale in the market.)

Several Japanese became naturalized (were given the rights of citizenship) in the Republic of Hawaii, but the U.S. territorial government refused to recognize them.

Asian American Population in 1900

Population category	Number
Total U.S. population	76,212,168
Total Asian American population	204,462
Chinese	118,746
Japanese	85,716

Source: U.S. Bureau of Census, Decennial Censuses of Population

April 29. Congress passed an act empowering the Immigration Commissioner to take charge of the administration of the Chinese Exclusion Act. *(Also see entry dated 1882.)*

April 30. The Organic Act, which established a U.S. territorial government in Hawaii, was signed into law by President William McKinley. Under this act, Chinese in Hawaii were required to apply for certificates of residence. However, whether they held certificates or not, they were prohibited from entering any other U.S. territory or the mainland.

The entry of all contract workers into Hawaii was made illegal. Immigrants had to prove that they were not under contract for specific labor, and that they carried at least $50 with them.

June 14. The Hawaiian Islands officially became a U.S. territory on this day, and all islanders became American citizens. President William McKinley appointed Sanford B. Dole the first governor (he had been serving as president of the Republic of Hawaii).

During this time period, the pineapple canning industry was established in Hawaii. A business venture of James D. Dole (cousin of Sanford Dole, territorial governor of Hawaii), Dole pineapple became a familiar product to mainland American households.

Some 60,000 Japanese immigrants were residing in the Hawaiian Islands, comprising nearly 40 percent of the total population. On the mainland, there were only 24,000 Japanese immigrants.

1901 Dr. Jokichi Takamine isolated pure epinephrine (adrenaline) at Johns Hopkins University. A longtime resident of the United States, Dr. Takamine declined honorary citizenship until all immigrants of Japanese ancestry were allowed the right to become citizens.

Congress passed an extension to what was commonly referred to as the "Chinese Exclusion Act," prohibiting Chinese from entering the country for yet another ten years. *(Also see entries dated 1882, 1892, and 1902.)*

California's anti-miscegenation law (prohibiting marriage between members of different races) was amended to bar marriages between whites and "Mongolians." This law remained in effect until November 1948.

Reverend Takie Okumura formed the first Japanese American baseball team, made up of students from his boarding school in Hawaii.

Jokichi Takamine III stands before a portrait of his grandfather, Dr. Jokichi Takamine

Baseball represented to the Japanese an opportunity to assimilate into (adapt to the customs of) American culture. It soon became a favorite sport of Japanese people in Hawaii and on the mainland, where many rival teams played each other.

January 9. Peter Ryu, the first recorded Korean immigrant to Hawaii, arrived on a Japanese ship, the *Kongkong Maru.*

July 4. William Howard Taft became the first civil governor of the Philippines.

1902   Congress passed "an act to prohibit the coming into and to regulate the residence within the United States, its territories and all territory under its jurisdiction, and the District of Columbia, of Chinese and persons of Chinese descent."

Congress indefinitely extended the prohibition of Chinese immigration and naturalization. Many Chinese, disgusted with the discriminatory legislation, returned to their homelands. *(Also see entry dated 1882.)*

White miners drove out Japanese immigrants employed at the Yukon Mining Company in Atkin, Alaska.

Two hundred thirty-four Chinese were illegally imprisoned in Boston, Massachusetts. Immigration officials and police, acting without search warrants, arrested those persons not carrying registration certificates as required by the Chinese Exclusion Act. *(Also see entry dated 1892.)*

The Hawaiian Sugar Planters' Association employed David W. Deshler in Korea to recruit Korean laborers.

Deshler, an American business executive with Japanese and Korean enterprises, was empowered by King Kojong of Korea to supervise the emigration of Korean laborers to Hawaii.

July 1. The U.S. Senate passed the Philippine Organic Act, which set up terms for the civil government established in 1901 under the governorship of William Howard Taft. The terms allowed for the greatest possible degree of self-government while maintaining U.S. rule. For example, political parties were allowed as long as they did not advocate independence. The legislature was bicameral (made up of two houses). The lower house was elected directly by districts of voters, but the upper house was appointed by the governor-general and had ultimate veto power. The United States maintained a majority in the upper house until 1913, when Governor-General Francis B. Harrison appointed a Filipino majority to it. *(Also see entry dated July 4, 1901.)*

December 22. The first group of Korean emigrants left Korea for Hawaii aboard the SS *Gaelic*.

1903   About 2,000 Japanese and Mexican sugar beet workers went on strike in Oxnard, California, and formed the first successful farmworkers' union. The

American Federation of Labor, however, refused to recognize a nonwhite union.

Seito Saibara, a former member of the Japanese Diet (parliament), settled near Houston to begin a rice-growing industry.

Korean Ahn Chang-ho established the Chinmok-hoe, or Friendship Society. *(Also see entry dated 1899.)*

January 13. One hundred Koreans arrived in Hawaii on the SS *Gaelic* and were inspected aboard the ship. Later, they were divided into small groups and sent to plantations. These early immigrants and those to come in the following months and years, were hired as agricultural workers in place of Chinese when the Chinese Exclusion Act took effect in Hawaii. Many of them were not experienced farm workers and subsequently moved to the mainland, often to work as railroad laborers. *(Also see entry dated 1882.)*

Two young Filipino men—participants in the pensionado program

August 26. Inspired by a plan devised by William Howard Taft, civil governor of the Philippines, the *pensionado* program was begun. Under this program, the American government provided aid to young Filipinos who wished to study in the United States.

November 3. A group of 100 young Filipinos arrived in California—the beginning of the pensionado program (see entry above). By 1912, 209 Filipino men and women had been educated under this program. It cost the U.S. government $479,940.

1904   Syngman Rhee (1875–1965), leader of the Independence Club in Korea, arrived in the United States. He proceeded to earn a bachelor's degree from George Washington University, a master's degree from Harvard University, and a doctorate in international law from Princeton University. He returned to Korea in 1910, only to flee to Hawaii a year later when Japan annexed (took over) Korea. There he organized the Korean Methodist Church and Korean Christian Institute, and later became principal of the Korean Boarding School. Also founder of the Comrade Society, he became a leader in the Korean indepedence movement. *(Also see entries dated 1911 and 1913.)*

Isamu Noguchi at the installation of his work "Bolt of Lightning," a Philadelphia memorial to Benjamin Franklin

Yamato (farming colony) founder Jo Sakai, with his wife, Sada, and daughters Tomoko, Yoshiko, and Chikako (pictured left to right) in 1915

Isamu Noguchi, Japanese American sculptor and architect, was born in Los Angeles to an American mother and a Japanese father.

Despite his growing stature as an artist, Noguchi voluntarily entered an internment camp in Arizona after the outbreak of World War II to show his outrage at the imprisonment of his fellow Japanese Americans. *(Also see entry dated February 19, 1942.)* He was held there for seven months. After the war, he entered the most prolific artistic period of his life.

Noguchi's career of five decades produced such works as *Red Cube* on the plaza of the Marine Midland Building in New York City, the *Billy Rose Sculpture Garden* in Jerusalem, Israel, *2 Peace Bridges* in Hiroshima, Japan, *Bolt of Lightning* in Philadelphia, and the sculpture garden at the Yale Beinecke Rare Book and Manuscript Library in New Haven, Connecticut.

Jo Sakai, an American-educated Japanese man, founded a Yamato (farming) colony near Boca Raton, Florida.

The colony struggled until 1906, when the first pineapple crop proved successful. But two years later, a blight (disease) struck the pineapple crops. This failure, in addition to growing competition from Cuban pineapples, brought an end to the colony.

September 23. Executive Order 38 was issued by the government of the Philippine Islands, applying U.S. government regulations concerning the exclusion of Chinese to the Philippines. *(Also see entry dated 1882.)*

1905

Japan had become more and more dominant in Korea at the turn of the century. In 1904, Japanese forces moved through Korea to attack Manchuria, a large section of China that shares its southern border with Korea. The Japanese troops never withdrew from Korea; in 1905 Japan declared Korea its virtual protectorate, meaning that Korea was to be a dependent state with Japan as its ruler, although there was not yet any formal recognition of this relationship.

Ting Chia Chen and Ying Shing Wen were the first Chinese to attend the U.S. Military Academy at West Point, New York. They graduated in 1909.

China launched a nationwide boycott against U.S. goods to protest U.S. discrimination and prejudice against Chinese.

The first Asian Indians arrived in Canada as contract workers,

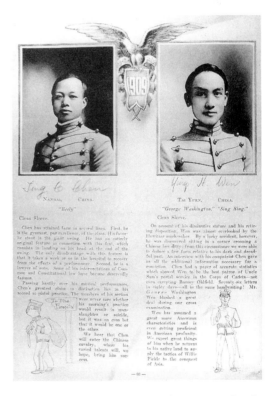

1909 U.S. Military Academy yearbook entries of first Chinese graduates

lured by Canadian companies' promises of great economic opportunities. Nearly 5,000 would arrive by 1908.

Nonetheless, the Canadian government sought to prevent Asian Indians from entering Canada by passing regulations stipulating that they must have come directly from India and not have resided in any other nation just prior to entering Canada. Many Indian emigrants who were turned away went south to the United States, specifically to Washington and Oregon.

The Korean Evangelical Society was organized in San Francisco.

Many Koreans had become Christians even before they left their homeland. After their arrival in the United States, they worked hard to convert other Koreans to Christianity.

The Mutual Assistance Society was established by Koreans in San Francisco. The society soon began publishing the first Korean-language newspaper.

February 10. The Korean Episcopal Church in Honolulu was founded.

Korean churches served not only the religious needs of their members but also provided a community meeting place away from the discrimination of the outside world. The Korean independence movement found its headquarters in local churches, where meetings were held and strategies prepared.

May 14. The Asiatic Exclusion League, a group made up of representatives of 67 labor organizations, was established in San Francisco. Eventually, more than 200 labor unions joined the league to restrict Asian immigration, working through the courts, through propaganda, and through violence.

1906 Hawaiian sugarcane companies began recruiting indentured workers from the Philippines. (Indentured workers were bound to work for a specified time period, especially in return for payment of travel expenses and maintenance at the location of the work.) By the late 1920s, Filipinos would become the largest group of Asians on the plantations.

Filipinos were particularly in demand because, as United States "nationals," they could travel with American passports, and existing immigration laws did not apply to them.

Filipino workers arrive in Hawaii

The San Francisco earthquake destroyed Chinatown.

This actually improved the circumstances of many Chinese immigrants because all municipal records were destroyed in the fires following the quake. Enterprising Chinese forged new documents claiming they were born in San Francisco. As citizens, they could bring their wives and children to the United States. Some Chinese posed as sons of these new "citizens" and immigrated based on the forged documents. These imposters came to be known as "paper sons."

A group of fifteen Filipino workers arrived in Hawaii to work for the Hawaiian Sugar Planters' Association.

The Yamato Colony of California was founded by Abiko Kyutaro in the central San Joaquin Valley. It was similar to the farming colony established in Boca Raton, Florida. Abiko was a labor contractor and newspaper publisher. *(Also see entry dated 1904.)*

35

July 18. Future U.S. Senator Samuel I. Hayakawa was born in Vancouver, British Columbia, Canada.

October 26. President Theodore Roosevelt sent Victor Metcalf (1884–1936) to San Francisco to confer with city officials on the question of school segregation.

November. The San Francisco School Board created an international incident when it ordered children of Chinese, Japanese, and Korean residents to attend the segregated Oriental Public School. There were 93 such children, 25 of whom were American citizens. Many of the children's parents protested the decision. *(Also see entry dated 1885.)*

December. Negotiations to restrict Japanese immigration began. They were carried out successfully, and a gentleman's agreement was reached between the United States and Japan in 1908. Japan agreed to stop issuing passports to Japanese laborers if the United States did not name the Japanese explicitly in the immigration laws.

1907 Recruitment intensified for single Filipino men to work in Alaskan fisheries and the growing agricultural industries of Hawaii and California. *(Also see entry dated 1906.)*

American-educated Jo Kamosu Sakai petitioned the state of Florida to incorporate the Yamato Colony Association, a settlement of Japanese farmers in southern Florida he founded to grow pineapples. *(Also see entry dated 1904.)*

Anna May Wong, America's first Asian American movie star, was born in Los Angeles, California.

Wong's fame rests on her portrayal of Hollywood's stereotypes of villainous Oriental women—the exotic slave girl, the dragon lady, the mysterious siren. Nonetheless, she vehemently protested against the limited and often offensive roles she was offered. She retired at age thirty-five, disgusted with the American motion picture industry, and devoted herself to the war effort (World War II) by working for the United China Relief Fund and touring with the United Service Organizations (USO). Wong died in her sleep in 1961.

January 17. A U.S. attorney filed a brief on behalf of Aoki Keikichi against the principal of San Francisco's Redding School to test the constitutionality of the segregation order issued by the San Francisco School Board. The case of *Aoki* v. *Deane* was dismissed after President Theodore Roosevelt intervened and forced the San Francisco School Board to rescind its segregation order. *(Also see entry dated 1885.)*

February 20. President Theodore Roosevelt signed a bill that further restricted Japanese immigration. *(Also see entry dated December 1906.)*

Anna May Wong

February 26. "The Regulation Governing the Admission of Chinese" outlined procedures for interrogating Chinese entering the United States.

March 14. On the basis of the February 20 immigration law, President Theodore Roosevelt issued Executive Order 589, which barred Japanese from entering the continental United States via Hawaii, Mexico, or Canada. In exchange for Roosevelt's intervention in the San Francisco school segregation case, Japan did not protest. *(Also see entries dated January 17, 1907, and February 20, 1907.)*

September 2. Representatives from 24 Korean organizations and village councils in Hawaii met and decided to create the United Korean Society, with headquarters in Honolulu and branches throughout the Hawaiian Islands.

October 1. Hiram Fong, the first Asian American to be elected to the U.S. Senate, was born in Honolulu, Hawaii, to Chinese immigrants.

Fong earned his J.D. (doctor of laws) from Harvard University in 1935 after having worked for his living since the age of four. After founding a law firm in Hawaii, he began a career in public service that led him to the Senate in 1959 as the first senator from the new state of Hawaii. He worked not only to benefit the state of Hawaii, but also to champion civil rights and minority appointments to the Senate. Fong retired from the Senate in 1977 to become founder and board member of several corporations.

October 22. The United Korean Society began publishing its newspaper, *United Korean News. (Also see entry dated September 2, 1907.)*

1908

Japanese serviceman Buntaro Kumagai, honorably discharged from the U.S. Army, was denied naturalization even though a law of 1862 allowed "any alien" honorably discharged from U.S. military service to apply for naturalization. Citizenship was denied on the grounds that the words "any alien" meant those who are "free white persons or those of African descent." *(Also see entries dated 1862 and 1910.)*

The Japanese Association of America was founded in San Francisco to counter racial discrimination. Prior to World War II, it was the most important institution in Japanese American communities. Among its other services, the Japanese Association of America hired European American lawyers to help fight such discriminatory measures as the alien land laws. *(Also see entry dated May 19, 1913.)*

March 23. Chang In-hwan (1875–1930), a Korean patriot, shot and killed an American, Durham Stevens, who supported the Japanese takeover of Korea as a protectorate (the relationship of superior authority assumed by one power or state over a dependent one).

May 23. The Korean Women's Association was established in San Francisco.

1909

Yung Wing, a Chinese American educated at Yale University, published his autobiography, *My Life in China and America. (Also see entry dated 1854.)*

Eight thousand Japanese sugar plantation workers went on strike on the island of Oahu, Hawaii. The strike was led by Fred Kinzaburo Makino, who was of Japanese and German heritage. This major strike for equal wages by Japanese workers in Hawaii lasted for four months, but did not fully achieve the results desired. Wages were eventually equalized, but the number of Japanese workers was reduced proportionately over the next several years.

February 1. California's Mutual Assistance Society and Hawaii's United Korean Society merged into one organization to work for Korea's independence from Japan. The new organization was called the Korean National Association and it began publishing a newspaper, *The New Korea. (Also see entries dated 1905 and September 2, 1907.)*

August 5. The Payne-Aldrich Tariff Act, which outlined a system of taxes on imports, went into effect. The Philippine Tariff Act also became effective on this day. On October 3, 1913, the Payne-Aldrich Act was replaced by the Underwood-Simmons Act, which established free trade between the Philippines and the United States. *(Also see entry dated October 3, 1913.)*

October 30. Channing Liem, Korean diplomat, scholar, and minister, was born in Ul Yul, a rural village.

After earning a college degree in Korea and a bacholor of science at Lafayette College in Pennsylvania, Liem entered the New York Theological Seminary and became pastor of New York City's Korean Church and Institute, at the time the only Korean church in the United States. He later earned his master's degree and Ph.D. and taught government and political theory at various colleges in the 1950s. In 1959 he helped form the new South Korean delegation to the United Nations. After leaving his government post, Liem became an international activist in support of democracy in his homeland and continued to pursue his dreams of the reunification of Korea (which had been divided into North Korea and South Korea in 1945).

1910 Twenty-seven anti-Japanese proposals were introduced by the California legislature. Governor Hiram Johnson, persuaded by President William Howard Taft, discouraged the legislature from approving these proposals.

Japanese picture brides arrived in the United States. The picture bride system was similar to the custom of arranged marriage in Japan; letters and pictures were exchanged until the woman could join her prospective husband in the United States.

Asian American Population in 1910

Population category	Number
Total U.S. population	92,228,531
Total Asian American population	249,926
Chinese	94,414
Filipino (from the Philippines)	2,767
Japanese	152,745
Korean	5,008

Source: U.S. Bureau of Census, Decennial Censuses of Population

Japan declared Korea its colony, making its takeover official. Korea remained a colony of Japan until 1945 when it was liberated by U.S. and Soviet troops at the end of World War II. *(Also see entry dated 1905.)*

Angel Island in San Francisco Bay, California, was set up as a point of entry and detention center for non-laboring Asian immigrants. Long waiting periods under inhumane conditions led some immigrants detained there to commit suicide.

The Supreme Court broadened the 1870 Naturalization Act to prohibit other Asians immigrants fron becoming citizens of the United States. The law originally targeted only Chinese. *(Also see entry dated 1870.)*

Arthur K. Ozawa, Hawaiian-born graduate of the University of Michigan Law School, was admitted to the bar in Michigan and Hawaii. He is believed to be the first Japanese American lawyer.

Namyo Bessho, of Japanese descent, was honorably discharged after five years in the U.S. Navy, but had his application for naturalization rejected. *(Also see entry dated 1862 and 1908.)*

October 10. Syngman Rhee returned to Korea after receiving a Ph.D. from Princeton University. He was the first Korean to receive such a degree from an American institution of higher learning. *(Also see entry dated 1904.)*

November 28. Sara Choe, married to Yi Nae-su, arrived in Hawaii. She was the first of 951 picture brides to come from Korea. *(Also see entry dated 1910.)*

Barracks at Angel Island Immigration Station

1911   Yi Bom-jin, Korean Minister to Russia, committed suicide to protest the Japanese seizure of Korea. He willed $3,000 to the Korean National Association to be used for its political work. *(Also see entry dated February 1, 1909.)*

Syngman Rhee fled Korea, which had been annexed by Japan, and went to Hawaii where he began organizing the Korean Methodist Church and the Korean Christian Institute.

When whites drove eleven Korean apricot workers out of Hemet, California, the Japanese consul general offered to assist the workers. Korean association leaders, however, were indignant and refused Japanese assistance. The Korean associations in California then banded together to assert their separate identity from the Japanese Americans. Since Japan took over Korea, many Koreans were angry at the Japanese nation.

February. Har Dayal (1884–1939), an Asian Indian political leader, arrived in the United States. He later worked toward India's independence from Great Britain. Dayal formed the Ghadr (literally, "revolution") Party in 1913 to seek support

41

for revolution in India. *(Also see entry dated November 1, 1913.)*

August. At an Amateur Athletic Union (AAU) swim meet held in Hawaii, Native Hawaiian Duke Kahanamoku broke the world record for the 100-yard free-style by 4.6 seconds. Mainland officials questioned the results, so Hawaiian locals raised funds to send Kahanamoku to Chicago, Illinois, where he swam for the first time in a pool. At the Olympic trials in Philadelphia, Pennsylvania, Kahanamoku won a spot on the Olympic team. *(Also see entries dated August 24, 1890, and Summer 1912.)*

September 24. José Nisperos, a Filipino American, was the first Asian/Pacific American to win the Congressional Medal of Honor. He was cited for valor while fighting at Lapurap, Basilan, the Philippines, during the Spanish-American War. Nisperos was badly wounded. His left arm was broken and he received several spear wounds to the body and could not stand. Nisperos continued to fire his rifle with one hand. His action helped to prevent the annihilation of his unit.

November 2. Carlos Bulosan, Filipino American writer and poet, was born in Binalonan, the Philippines.

Duke Kahanamoku

Bulosan migrated to Seattle, Washington, as a young man. Alternately working at menial jobs and serving as a union organizer, he discovered writing as he passed long hours in the library between jobs, reading voraciously.

Bulosan's autobiography and most famous work, *America Is in the Heart,* was a critical success at the time it was published in 1946, but after Bulosan's death in 1956 of tuberculosis, his work was largely forgotten. His poetry, articles, and novels were brought to prominence in the 1970s by a new generation of Asian Americans hungry to learn about their history. *(Also see entry dated 1930.)*

1912 **January 1.** The Republic of China was founded by Sun Yat-sen (1866–1925), who became its first president.

Sun was the symbol and leader of the Chinese nationalist revolution (which aimed at moving the country from dictatorial dynastic rule to democracy). He first publicized his ideas in 1907 and continued to promote his revolutionary agenda and raise money from overseas supporters until the revolution broke out in 1911.

Summer. At the Olympic games in Stockholm, Sweden, Native Hawaiian swimmer Duke Kahanamoku tied the world record in a qualifying heat for the 100-meter freestyle. He went on to win the Gold Medal in the event. *(Also see entry dated August 1911.)*

September 16. The Korean Youth Corps, which established a voluntary program offering military training, in Hastings, Nebraska, under the leadership of Park Yong-man (1881–1928), graduated its first class of 13 students. Park Yong-man was an activist in the Korean independence movement who believed in the military training of Koreans in the United States.

1913 The Korean Boarding School changed its name to the Central Institute, and Syngman Rhee became its principal. *(Also see entry dated 1904.)*

Also that year, Rhee started a community organization, the Tongji-hoe (Comrade Society), to create a base of power for himself in the Korean independence movement. In another milestone of 1913, Ahn Chang-ho founded the Hung Sa Dang (Young Koreans Academy). *(Also see entry dated 1899.)*

May 13. The Corps for the Advancement of Individuals was organized by Koreans in America. Ahn Chang-ho served as chair of the board of directors. *(Also see entry dated 1899.)*

May 19. The California legislature passed the Alien Land Act and it was signed into law. According to the statute, a person ineligible for U.S. citizenship was forbidden to purchase land for agricultural purposes and could lease property for no more than three years. Similar laws were adopted in Washington, Oregon, Idaho, Montana, Arizona, New Mexico, Nebraska, Texas, Kansas, Louisiana, Missouri, and Minnesota.

June. Fifteen Korean fruit pickers, who had been hired by an orchard owner in Riverside County, California, were surrounded and driven off by a crowd of angry unemployed European Americans when they arrived at the train station.

October 3. The Underwood-Simmons Act, establishing free trade between the United States and the Philippines, replaced the Payne-Aldrich Tariff Act. *(Also see entry dated August 5, 1909)*

November 1. The Hindu Association was established under the leadership of Har Dayal, a founder of the Ghadr Party in San Francisco. *(Also see entry dated February 1911.)*

Hinduism is one of the oldest still-practiced religions/philosophies in the world. Although there is no single founder of the religion, it is distinctive in two main features: its *caste* system—a division of people into hereditary social classes that restricts the type of work and the social relations of each class's members—and the acceptance of the *Veda* as the most sacred scripture. Some of the deities of the Hindu religion are Vishnu and his early embodiments Rama and Krishnu, Shiva, and the elephant-headed god Ganesha. All of these gods are viewed as different forms of the one Supreme Being. Hinduism has many sects and has undergone continual transformation in its long history. Modern Hindu leaders are primarily interested in creating a better social world through spiritual enlightenment.

1914   **June 10.** The Korean Military Corps was organized by Park Yong-man, who believed that Korea's independence would come only if Japan were defeated militarily.

1915   Duke Kahanamoku, Gold Medalist in the 100-meter freestyle at the 1912 Olympics, caused a sensation when he visited Australia for a surfing exhibition. *(Also see entries dated August 24, 1890, August 1911, and Summer 1912.)*

Hearst newspapers reported, "Japan Plans to Invade and Conquer the U.S.," a sensational story that launched an anti-Japanese campaign.

March 11. *The New Korea* newspaper was printed on an Intertype machine, invented by Yi Dae-wi. *(Also see entry dated February 1, 1909.)*

October 15. Mike Masaoka, future national secretary for the Japanese American Citizens League, was born. *(Also see entry dated April 1929.)*

Senator Spark Matsunaga

1916 **October 8.** Future U.S. Senator Spark M. Matsunaga was born in Kauai, Hawaii.

Spark Masayuki Matsunaga was a leader in the 1988 Senate campaign to award war reparations to his fellow Japanese Americans who had been interned in "relocation centers" during World War II. During the war, Matsunaga had been a member of the highly decorated 100th Infantry Battalion of the U.S. Army; he received the Bronze Star Medal with Valor, Purple Heart with Oak Leaf Cluster, Army Commendation Medal, and five Battle Stars. *(Also see entry dated March 2, 1942.)*

1917 When Asian Indian laborers began to be perceived as a threat to white laborers, strict immigration restrictions were enforced against this new "Indian Menace." Pleas and petitions were ineffective, so Indians began seeking radical counsel by joining hands with Har Dayal and his Ghadr Party. Har Dayal led an Indian protest delegation at the congressional hearings of a bill intended to exclude all Asian immigrants. He was arrested and deportation proceedings were started against him. Har Dayal then surfaced in Germany, where an Indian Committee of National Independence had been formed. Some 400 other Indians also left the United States on Ghadr-organized missions, most of which failed. By 1917, the Ghadr movement had more or less collapsed in America. *(Also see entry dated February 1911.)*

The Selective Service Act was enacted as law. Under this act, men were required to register for military service on their eighteenth birthday. This registration created the "military draft," in which soldiers had no choice but to report for their military assignment.

February 5. The Asiatic Barred Zone Act became effective on this date. President Woodrow Wilson had vetoed the bill passed by Congress on December 14, 1916, but Congress overrode his veto. The Act precluded immigration from all of Asia and India by drawing an imaginary line from the Red Sea in the Middle East all the way through the Ural Mountains (the traditional boundary between Europe and Asia); people living east of the line were denied entry to the United States.

March 6. Ram Chandra, who worked with Har Dayal for India's independence, was tried in the the Hindu Conspiracy case. He was shot to death in the courtroom on April 23, 1918. *(Also see entries dated February 1911 and 1917.)*

April 26. Future architect I. M. (Ieoh Ming) Pei was born in Canton, China.

Pei arrived in San Francisco at the age of seventeen, intending to study architecture at an American university, but he transferred to the Massachusetts Institute of Technology to study engineering. The faculty there recognized his talent and persuaded him to reconsider the study of architecture; he graduated in 1940 and later earned a master's degree in architecture at Harvard University.

Pei went on to become one of the great architects of the modern era and is considered the dean of the modernist school of architecture. He has designed some of the world's most prominent buildings, including the addition to the Louvre museum in Paris, the East Wing of the National Gallery of Art in Washington, D.C., the John F. Kennedy Library in Boston, the Jacob Javits Center in New York City, the Fragrant Hill Hotel In Beijing, China, the Dallas, Texas, City Hall, and the Rock and Roll Hall of Fame in Cleveland, Ohio.

June. Twenty-nine thousand *issei* (Japanese immigrants), and some *nisei* (children of Japanese immigrants), registered for Selective Service in the Territory of Hawaii during World War I (1914–18).

November 21. The Japanese Boys Club and Japanese Girls Club were founded by Nellie Grace Oliver, a Caucasian (white) schoolteacher. They were the first social clubs established for nisei youth.

1918   A Yamato (farming) Colony was established in Cressy, California, by Abiko Kyutaro. *(Also see entry dated 1906.)*

The Hindustani Welfare Reform Society was established in the Imperial Valley, California, by members of three Asian Indian faiths—Sikh, Muslim, and Hindu—in order to transcend some of their differences.

July 29. The New Church, led by Syngman Rhee, was established by Koreans in Hawaii. *(Also see entry dated 1904.)*

1919   The American Loyalty Club was organized in San Francisco by a small group of *nisei* (children of Japanese immigrants). The club was started to coordinate efforts to demonstrate Japanese American national loyalty and the legitimate status of Japanese Americans as Americans, and to counter anti-Japanese American sentiment.

The Korean independence movement and the news of its brutal suppression by Japan energized Korean American churches and study groups to redouble aid. *(Also see entry dated March 1, 1919.)*

A provisional (temporary) Korean government-in-exile was set up in Shanghai, China, by expatriate Korean leaders.

A Yamato (farming) Colony was established in Cortez, California, by Abiko Kyutaro. *(Also see entry dated 1906.)*

March 1. Koreans in Korea protested Japanese colonial rule with a nonviolent nationwide demonstration. Many Koreans were killed by Japanese police. News of this protest, which began the Korean independence movement, reached Koreans in Hawaii and the mainland United States on March 9. The Korean National Association launched a fund-raising campaign for independence and collected $10,000. *(Also see entry dated February 1, 1909.)*

April 14–16. In Philadelphia, 150 Koreans attended the first Korean Liberty Congress, designed to draw the world's attention to the plight of Koreans in Japan-dominated Korea.

Asian American Population in 1920

Population category	Number
Total U.S. population	106,021,568
Total Asian American population	332,432
Chinese	85,202
Filipino (from the Philippines)	26,634
Japanese	220,596
Korean	6,181

Source: U.S. Bureau of Census, Decennial Censuses of Population

September. Valentine Stuart McClatchy (1857–1938), a publisher, formed the California Joint Immigration Committee and used it to drum up support for his anti-Japanese activities.

1920   Led by the Filipino Federation of Labor, plantation workers of Japanese and Filipino ancestry went on strike for six months in Hawaii demanding higher wages and better working conditions.

Duke Kahanamoku broke his own world record for the 100-meter freestyle at the Olympic Games in Antwerp, Belgium, just in time for his 30th birthday. *(Also see entries dated August 24, 1890, August 1911, Summer 1912, and 1915.)*

Women in the United States won the constitutional right to vote.

Agricultural entrepreneurs Charles Ho Kim and Kim Hyong-sun established the Kim Brothers Company in Reedley, California. Kim Hyong-sun and an employee named Anderson developed the nectarine, a cross between a peach and a plum.

A special act directed at Chinese women denied them automatic citizenship if they married an American citizen.

January 19. The California Alien Land Act of 1913 was amended to close loopholes in the original law. The revised edict prohibited Asian immigrant parents from serving as guardians of property for their minor citizen children and prohibited any leasing of land to aliens. *(Also see entry dated May 19, 1913.)*

February 20. The School of Aviation was founded in Willows, California, when Kim Chong-nim, a successful Korean American rice farmer known as the "rice king," donated three airplanes. Future pilots were to be trained there to fight against the Japanese empire in the Korean struggle for independence from Japan.

1921

The *Philippine Independent News*, the first Filipino newspaper in the continental United States, was published in Salinas, California.

Picture bride immigration ended after the United States convinced the Japanese government to stop issuing passports to prospective brides. *(Also see entry dated 1910.)*

Fifty-eight Japanese immigrant laborers in Turlock, California, were forcibly removed from the community and warned never to return.

There were about 1,000 immigrant Japanese mining coal in central Utah.

A Yamato Colony was started as a sugar plantation in Texas. The crop thrived, but the post-World War I economic depression caused its ultimate failure a few years later. Its sister colony near Boca Raton, Florida, experienced similar crop success, but economic challenges. *(Also see entry dated 1904.)*

January 22. The Caballeros de Dimas-Alang was established in San Francisco as a fraternal organization of Filipinos.

May 19. President Warren G. Harding signed the nation's first quota immigration act into law, limiting the number of immigrants from each country. It eventually led to the 1924 National Origins Act. *(Also see entry dated May 26, 1924.)*

The Seattle Progressive Citizens League was established by *nisei* Americans (children of Japanese immigrants) to fight racial discrimination.

July 7. The Comrade Society was organized, led by Syngman Rhee. *(Also see entries dated 1904 and 1913.)*

Railroad depot at Yamato Colony, Florida

1922   **September 22.** Congress passed the Cable Act, which revoked the American citizenship of any woman who married an alien ineligible for U.S. citizenship. Women of European or African ancestry could regain their citizenship—if they divorced their alien husbands or if the husbands died—through the process of naturalization, but Asian women could not since they were not eligible for naturalization themselves.

November 13. In *Takao* v. *United States* the Supreme Court upheld the Naturalization Act, which meant that aliens (specifically Japanese and other Asian immigrants) were ineligible for citizenship and thus could not be naturalized. *(Also see entry dated 1790.)*

Ozawa Takao had graduated from high school in California, attended college there, married an American-educated woman, and spoke only English in his home. Even so, he was denied citizenship because he was not white.

1923 A certificate of naturalization obtained in 1921 by Tokutaro Nishimura Slocum was revoked. Slocum was a sergeant major with the 82d Division in France during World War I and was severely wounded. He continued to fight for his right to citizenship. *(Also see entry dated 1935.)*

February 19. In the case of *United States* v. *Bhagat Singh Thind*, the Supreme Court declared Asian Indians ineligible for U.S. citizenship. The decision was based on an interpretation of the 1790 Naturalization Act. According to the decision, as an Asian Indian, Thind was not considered eligible for citizenship because he was not a "white man." *(Also see entries dated 1790 and November 13, 1922.)*

March 5. The American Loyalty Club of Fresno was organized, with Thomas Yatabe as president. This was the precursor to the Japanese American Citizens League. *(Also see entries dated April 1919 and 1929.)*

1924 Swimmer Duke Kahanamoku suffered his first defeat at the Olympic Games in Paris, France, when he was beaten by 19-year-old Johnny Weissmuller, who went on to play Tarzan in several Hollywood movies. Kahanamoku, a Native Hawaiian, won the Silver Medal, and his brother, Sam, won the Bronze.

Japan changed its nationality law so that children born in the United States to Japanese parents were not considered Japanese nationals, unless parents specifically registered the child as such at a Japanese consulate within 14 days of his or her birth. The law also allowed children born prior to 1924 to renounce their Japanese nationality.

February 2. A U.S. branch of the Legionarios del Trabajo, Inc. was organized in San Francisco. The organization, founded in Manila, the Philippines, in 1916 after a strike at the Manila Electric Company, was styled after American fraternal organizations.

May 26. President Calvin Coolidge signed into law the Immigration Act of 1924, also known as the Quota Immigration or National Origins Act. It excluded the immigration of all Asian laborers, except for Filipinos, who were already U.S. nationals because the Philippines was a U.S. protectorate. *(Also see entry dated May 19, 1921.)*

September 7. Future U.S. Senator Daniel Inouye was born in Honolulu, Hawaii.

Daniel Ken Inouye was the first Japanese American to serve in the United States Congress, starting in the House of Representatives and then moving to the Senate as a representative from Hawaii. He also became a member of the Senate Watergate Committee, which investigated wrongdoing in Richard M. Nixon's 1972 presidential campaign.

During World War II, Inouye enlisted in the army and was assigned to the famous all-Japanese American 442d Regimental Combat Team. At the close of the war, Inouye was severely injured by a bullet to the stomach, yet he managed to stifle an enemy machine gun nest while receiving further serious injuries to his arm and leg. He was made a captain for this display of bravery and was awarded a Distinguished Service Cross, a Bronze Star, a Purple Heart with Cluster, and twelve other medals and citations.

Daniel K. Inouye, a soldier and hero in World War II

1925   A district court in Massachusetts approved naturalization for Hidemitsu Toyota, who served in the U.S. Coast Guard from 1913 to 1923. The Court of Appeals, however, cancelled his certificate of citizenship, and the U.S. Supreme Court upheld the cancellation, ruling that he was ineligible for citizenship because he was neither white nor black. (*Also see entries dated 1790 and November 13, 1922.*)

May 25. The Supreme Court ruled on the case of *Chang Chan et al.* v. *John D. Nagle*, declaring that Chinese wives of United States citizens were not allowed to come to the United States in accordance with the Immigration Act of 1924. *(Also see entry dated May 26, 1924.)*

Previously, both U.S.-born and immigrant Chinese were allowed to bring their wives and families to the United States. The Immigration Act of 1924, however, had aimed at preventing Chinese people from having families in the United States. *Chang Chan et al* v. *John D. Nagle* challenged the 1924 act, but the Supreme Court ruled that Chinese wives of U.S. born citizens were not entitled to residence. As a result, the Chinese population continued to have many more men than women until the early 1960s.

1926   The China Institute in America, Inc. was founded to promote cultural understanding between China and the United States.

1927   The Supreme Court upheld the ruling of the Circuit Court of Appeals on the case of *Weedin* v. *Chin Bow* and declared that a person born abroad of an American parent or parents who has never lived in the United States cannot be a citizen of the United States.

James Sakamoto (1903–1955), who would go on to be an important figure in the development of the Japanese American Citizens League, became the first *nisei* boxer to fight professionally at the Madison Square Garden Coliseum in New York City. *(Also see entry dated April 1929.)*

During the American Federation of Labor's annual convention, delegates resolved to encourage Congress to prohibit Filipino immigration.

The Filipino Federation of Labor was founded in Los Angeles. Its purpose was to protect migrant workers from abuse by farm owners and labor contractors.

1928   Asian Indian American Dhan Gopal Mukerji published *Gay-Neck, The Story of a Pigeon,* which won the prestigious Newbery Award. The book was also named by the American Institute of Graphic Arts as one of the fifty best books of the year.

January 1. The *Japanese American Courier* was published by James Sakamoto in Seattle, Washington. *(Also see entry dated 1927.)*

May 18. House Bill 13,900 was introduced by Congressman Richard J. Welch and Senator Hiram Johnson of California. The bill was designed to exclude Filipinos from the United States.

June 29. *The Samil Sinbo* (news) was published by a group of Korean students in New York. Among them were Chang Dok-su, Yun Ch'i-yong, and Ho Chung, all of whom would play major roles in South Korean politics after the end of World War II (1939–45).

September 18. A *nisei* teenager named Myles Fukunaga kidnapped and murdered ten-year-old Gill Jamieson, son of the vice-president of the Hawaiian Trust Company, the landlord of Fukunaga's family. The murder had been planned as revenge against the company for demanding a twenty-dollar payment the Fukunagas could not make. Fukunaga was subsequently hanged for the crime.

GAY-NECK
THE STORY OF A PIGEON
BY
DHAN GOPAL MUKERJI

AWARDED THE

JOHN NEWBERY MEDAL

ILLUSTRATED BY
BORIS ARTZYBASHEFF

Cover of *Gay-Neck, The Story of a Pigeon*

1929

February 28. Philippine Labor Commissioner Cayetano Ligot recommended to the Hawaiian legislature that Filipinos be prevented from coming to Hawaii unless they had guaranteed jobs or sufficient funds with which to return home.

April. Kido Saburo, Thomas Yatabe, and Clarence Arai proposed the establishment of the Japanese American Citizens League (JACL). It was formally established in 1930. *(Also see entry dated March 5, 1923.)*

JACL members believed that the best way to prove themselves as legitimate Americans to the European Americans was to espouse the American ideals of individualism, free enterprise, and private property ownership.

Asian American Population in 1930

Population category	Number
Total U.S. population	123,202,660
Total Asian American population	489,326
Chinese	102,159
Filipino (from the Philippines)	108,424
Japanese	278,743
Korean	8,332

Source: U.S. Bureau of Census, Decennial Censuses of Population

The Japanese Amateur Athletic Union (JAAU) was founded in the San Francisco Bay area.

1930   Carlos Bulosan, who would become one of the most famous Filipino American writers and activists, paid $75 to sail from the Philippines to Seattle in steerage. (Steerage is the part of a passenger ship where passengers travel at the cheapest rate. Living conditions in steerage typically offered little privacy. Passengers were crowded into cramped quarters below deck.) At the time Bulosan arrived in the United States, the country was entering a deep economic downturn, the Great Depression. *(Also see entry dated November 2, 1911.)*

The Great Depression caused an increase in anti-Asian attacks and riots, especially against Filipinos, who were concentrated in agricultural "stoop labor" (so called because planting crops involved much stooping over). The outbreaks of violence against Asian immigrants were probably due to the efforts of racist European Americans to find scapegoats for their problems.

Kang Younghill (1903–1972) published *The Grass Roof*, which was well received by the U.S. public.

The U.S. Census counted 45,208 Filipinos and Filipino Americans in the 48 continental United States. The actual figure was probably higher.

January 10. In the western California town of Pajaro (near Watsonville), the Northern Monterrey Chamber of Comerce passed an anti-Filipino resolution.

The aim of the resolution was to discourage the hiring of Filipino workers. During the Depression, racist sentiment against all immigrant workers flared. Millions of unemployed people were struggling to find jobs, and immigrant workers sometimes became scapegoats for the country's economic hardships. Filipinos in the Watsonville area were outraged, and responded with pamphlets and newspaper articles. Emotions ran high, leading to unrest at a dance hall leased by Filipinos. Whites, who were not admitted to the hall, gathered in increasing numbers outside. Violent encounters in the streets over the course of several days culminated on January 22.

January 22. Fermin Tober was killed during an anti-Filipino riot in Watsonville, California (see entry above). Over 500 youths participated in several days of violence in an attempt to drive Filipinos out of the area. This unrest came to be known as "The Watsonville Riots." Seven suspects were arrested, but none were convicted of any crime.

The Great Depression

In October 1929, the U.S. stock market crashed. This triggered a serious and lengthy downturn in the economy. Many companies went out of business. Banks collapsed, wiping out the personal savings of millions of people. By 1933, 12 million men and women had lost their jobs. There were no government programs, such as unemployment insurance, in operation then. Unemployed people had to rely on private charities, religious organizations, friends, and family members to get the basic necessities of life—including food, fuel for heating, clothing, and medical care. Franklin Delano Roosevelt was inaugurated as president in March 1933. During his administration, programs—often called "New Deal" programs—were instituted to relieve the stresses of unemployment. ⊙

February 26. Los Angeles Superior Court Judge J. K. Smith ruled that Filipinos were members of the "Mongolian" race. This opened the way for the invalidation of more than 100 interracial marriages performed since 1921.

August 29. The Japanese American Citizens League, formed to focus on educational issues and civil rights, held its first national convention in Seattle. *(Also see entry dated April, 1929.)*

1931   The Cable Act was amended, allowing American women to retain their citizenship after marriage to aliens ineligible for U.S. citizenship. *(Also see entry dated September 22, 1922.)*

The India Society of America was founded by Hari G. Govil in New York.

Bruno Lasker was commissioned to study Filipino immigration to Hawaii and the United States.

September 18. Japan invaded Manchuria, a region in northeastern China.

November 12. U.S. Congressman Norman Y. Mineta was born in San Jose, California.

In 1942, the Mineta family was relocated to an internment camp in Wyoming, where they spent three years during World War II. Mineta's father was deeply wounded by what he felt was his betrayal by his beloved country. Mineta never forgot the pain that thousands of Japanese Americans endured, and, in the historic 100th Congress in 1987, he and another Japanese American congressman introduced their plan for redress. They convinced Congress to approve a measure that included an official apology from the government and a $1.2 billion award to be divided among the Japanese Americans who had been forced from their homes. *(Also see entry dated February 19, 1942.)*

Norman Y. Mineta

Prior to this, Mineta had become the first Japanese American mayor of an American city— San Jose, California. He was elected in 1971.

1932   In response to the Japanese occupation of Manchuria, U.S. Secretary of State Henry Stimson declared that the United States would not recognize territorial claims prompted by means of force. Chinese in the United States supported this policy and rendered financial support to Manchurian efforts to resist the Japanese.

Chinese tong wars erupted in the United States. Tongs were formed to be mutual aid societies, but they often developed into organized crime syndicates that settled territorial disputes with violence.

The Japanese Athletic Union was formed to help regulate the YMCA sports leagues that had sprung up in Los Angeles.

1933   Adolf Hitler was named Chancellor of the Third Reich, a National Socicalist (Nazi) dictatorship of Germany.

November 30. The Filipino Labor Union was founded; by the end of the year, it had established a number of branch offices in central California.

1934   The *nisei* Central Japanese (baseball) League was formed with eight teams in central California.

March 24. President Franklin D. Roosevelt signed the Tydings-McDuffie Act, which prohibited Filipino immigration. The Act declared the Philippines a separate state or commonwealth, although it stipulated that true independence was not to occur for ten years after the passage of the bill. Thus all foreign-born Filipinos became aliens, not nationals as they had been previously considered. Filipino immigration was restricted to 50 per year. This resulted in the separation of many families.

August 27. The Salinas Lettuce Strike, led by the Filipino Labor Union, was called against the Central California Vegetable Growers and Shippers' Association.

October 8. Syngman Rhee married an Austrian woman, Francesca Donner, and drew a great deal of criticism from the Korean Hawaiian community because she was white. *(Also see entry dated 1904.)*

1935 Seiji Ozawa was born in Shen-yang, China. Ozawa, who became the music director of the Boston Symphony Orchestra in 1973, began his music career in Japan. He continued his studies in Europe and the United States, where he eventually caught the eye of New York Philharmonic conductor and composer Leonard Bernstein. Bernstein appointed him assistant conductor of the New York Philharmonic for the 1961–62 season. During the 1960s, Ozawa conducted many of the world's major orchestras. He was appointed artistic director of the Tanglewood Festival, summer home of the Boston Symphony Orchestra, in 1970. His appointment to the position of music director of the Boston

Seiji Ozawa

Symphony Orchestra came three years later, a post he held as of 1995.

After years of campaigning for the restoration of his naturalized U.S. citizenship, Tokutaro Nishimura Slocum finally succeeded. The congressional bill that restored his U.S. citizenship also granted citizenship to approximately 500 Asians who had served honorably in the U.S. armed forces during World War I. *(Also see entry dated 1923.)*

July 10. The Filipino Repatriation Act was signed into law, allowing Filipinos in the United States to go back to the Philippine Islands at U.S. government expense. Once there, however, they could only return to the United States as part of the annual quota. *(Also see entry dated March 24, 1934.)*

August 17. The government of the Philippine Commonwealth was formalized and Manuel Luis Quezon y Molina (1878–1944) was elected president. *(Also see entry dated March 24, 1934.)*

59

1936
Zubin Mehta was born April 29, 1936, in Bombay, India. He would go on to become a world-famous conductor of symphony orchestras. His father was a cofounder of the Bombay Symphony, so the young Mehta was exposed to music at an early age. At sixteen, he was conducting the orchestra while his father was away on tour. By the time he was eighteen, Mehta had abandoned his other studies to pursue conducting as a career. *(Also see entry dated 1962.)*

In a bloody rebellion, Japanese Army officers tried to take over the Japanese government. The rebels surrendered only when Emperor Hirohito himself appealed to them to put down their arms.

Zubin Mehta

The Cable Act of 1922 was repealed. *(Also see entries dated September 22, 1922, and 1931.)*

Ahn Ik-t'ae (1906–1965), a Korean composer in Philadelphia, completed his composition of the Korean national anthem.

The Congress of Industrial Organizations (CIO) admitted workers of Japanese ancestry and other nonwhites into mainstream organized labor.

November 25. Japan joined Germany in an Anti-Comintern (communist) Pact opposing the Soviet Union.

Italy joined the pact with Germany and Japan a year later. (Communism is a political doctrine in which members of a community enjoy common ownership of all property and material provision for all according to need. Communists also believe that a state-run economy is superior to private enterprise and that land should be organized for communal cultivation.)

December. Chiang Kai-shek, the Nationalist leader of the majority of China, was kidnapped in the province of Xi'an, China.

When Japan invaded Manchuria in 1931, Chiang had decided not to regain the region. He felt it necessary first to attack China's growing Communist movement, which had established a republic in the southwest region of the country. Although Chiang's attack was fierce and thousands of Communists were killed, Chiang could not effectively crush the movement. The Communists appealed to Chiang to stop the civil war and direct his forces against the Japanese invaders, but he refused. Finally, he was kidnapped by a Chinese warlord who was sympathetic to the Communists and would not let Chiang go until he agreed to halt attacks against the Communists.

1937

One of the first sociological studies on Koreans in Hawaii was completed by Bernice B. H. Kim at the University of Hawaii.

The United States broke off commercial relations with Japan.

July 7. Full-scale war broke out between Japan and China. By the next year, Chiang Kai-shek had lost all of eastern China. A million Japanese occupied eight provinces, including every harbor along the coastline. Because the Japanese controlled the most fertile farmland in the country, Chiang's Nationalist government seized the food of the poorest peasants, leaving five million Chinese to starve. Many concerned Chinese in the United States sent financial contributions to help China repel Japanese aggression.

October 21. Haan Kil-soo, a Korean resident of Hawaii, testified before a Congressional State Committee that the Japanese government was attempting to unite Asians in Hawaii in opposition to the whites.

1938

Hiram Fong was elected to the legislature of the Territory of Hawaii. Fong, the son of a Chinese immigrant sugar plantation laborer, worked tirelessly toward Hawaii's statehood. *(Also see entry dated October 1, 1907.)*

April 28. President Franklin D. Roosevelt issued a proclamation establishing immigration quotas for each country in "compliance with the pertinent provisions of the Immigration Act of 1924." *(Also see entry dated May 26, 1924.)*

This proclamation set limits for specific numbers of immigrants from nearly 70 countries. The immigration quotas ranged from 100 for China, India, and Japan, to 65,721 for Great Britain, 17,853 for Ireland, and 27,370 for Germany.

1939 Korean Americans picketed in Los Angeles against U.S. scrap iron and airplane fuel shipments to Japan. This was the first public demonstration in the United States against Japan's invasion of China. (Japan was also in control of Korea at the time.)

The Japanese American 3YSC (Three Year Swim Club), organized among the Hawaiian plantations by teacher Soichi Sakamoto, won its first national team swim title at the national meet in Detroit, Michigan.

The star of the team was Kiyoshi "Keo" Nakama, who won his first national title in the 200-meter freestyle. He would go on to win 27 NCAA (National Collegiate Athletic Association), Big Ten (college), and AAU (Amateur Athletic Union) titles and would coach the U.S. Olympic and University of Hawaii swim teams.

The Intermountain District Council of the Japanese American Citizens League was organized by Mike Masaoka. *(Also see entry dated October 15, 1915.)*

1940 President Franklin D. Roosevelt declared an embargo (prohibition of shipment) on most goods to Japan.

The Metropolitan Museum of Art in New York City acquired a painting by Chinese American watercolorist Dong Kingman. This purchase was the first acquisition by the esteemed museum of any work by an Asian American artist.

March 9. Leaders of the Japanese American Citizens League met with the Los Angeles City Council and assured council members of their loyalty to the United States in the face of increasing Japanese aggression abroad. *(Also see entry dated April 1929.)*

March 21. Leaders of the Japanese American Citizens League met with officials of the Army and Navy Intelligence Service and pledged to their loyalty and cooperation. *(Also see entry dated April 1929.)*

Asian American Population in 1940

Population category	Number
Total U.S. population	132,212,168
Total Asian American population	489,984
Chinese	106,334
Filipino (from the Philippines)	98,535
Japanese	285,115
Korean	8,568

Source: U.S. Bureau of Census, Decennial Censuses of Population

June. Congress passed the Alien Registration Act, which required that all aliens aged fourteen and older living in the U.S. must register with the Justice Department.

September. Germany, Japan, and Italy signed the Tripartite Pact, committing each of them to wage war against any nation that attacked any one of them.

Franklin D. Roosevelt was re-elected to an unprecedented third term as president of the United States.

September 7. Haan Kil-soo, leader of the Sino-Korean People's League ("Sino" denotes China; China and Korea were united in opposition to Japan), urged Koreans registering as aliens in Hawaii to do so as Koreans and not as Japanese subjects. At the time, Korea was part of the Japanese Empire. *(Also see entry dated June 1940.)*

November 27. Bruce Lee, Chinese American actor and martial arts master, was born in San Francisco.

After Bruce was born, the Lee family returned to Hong Kong, where Lee grew up a street-wise ruffian involved in gangs. Yet the graceful Lee became an expert dancer and began to study kung fu, a traditional martial art. He eventually developed his own martial arts technique based on kung fu and philosophy. He began to star in films in Hong Kong. His reputation as a film star helped him to start his own school of martial arts in Seattle, and eventually to achieve Hollywood stardom as a martial arts fighter. Throughout his life, though, Lee was denied roles because of prevailing anti-Asian sentiment; when Caucasian actor David Carradine was cast in the television series *Kung Fu*, Lee protested the decision by returning to Hong Kong. He died a mysterious death in 1973, leaving his mark on the world as an action film superstar and a legend in the martial arts world.

1941   Haan Kil-soo charged that Japan planned to attack the United States and that the Japanese in Hawaii were ready to assist Japan in case of war with the United States. *(Also see entry dated September 7, 1940.)*

Japanese troops occupied Indonesia.

Voluntary enlistment of Asian Americans into the U.S. armed forces began. *Nisei* (children of Japanese immigrants) volunteers came from Hawaii and later from the internment camps. *(Also see entry dated February 19, 1942.)*

Kido Saburo (1902–1977), president of the Japanese American Citizens League, sent a telegram to President Franklin D. Roosevelt pledging the loyalty and cooperation of the *nisei*. *(Also see entry dated April 1929.)*

February 2. Upon his arrival in the United States, Japanese Ambassador Admiral Kichisaburo Nomura urged all Japanese Americans to remain loyal and true to the United States.

May 9. The Japanese American Creed, written by Japanese American Citizens League leader Mike Masaoka was published in the Congressional Record. *(Also see entry dated October 15, 1915.)*

July. President Franklin D. Roosevelt placed an embargo on the shipment of petroleum products to Japan. To impede Japan's war effort, the British and Dutch imposed similar sanctions, effectively cutting off Japan's oil supply.

July 26. The United States abrogated (made invalid) its treaty of commerce and friendship with Japan and froze the assets of Japanese nationals in the United States.

October 16. In Japan, the civilian government of Prince Fumimaro Konoye fell and was replaced by a military cabinet headed by General Hideki Tojo.

November. A report prepared by Chicago businessman Curtis B. Munson and submitted to the president and secretary of state certified that Japanese Americans possessed an extraordinary degree of loyalty to the United States, and that immigrant Japanese were of no danger to the United States. Years of secret surveillance by the Federal Bureau of Investigation (FBI) and Office of Naval Intelligence corroborated the report.

November 25. Japan's naval fleet sailed for Hawaii.

December 7. In a surprise attack, Japan bombed Pearl Harbor, in Hawaii (Hawaii was then a territory of the United States). Pearl Harbor had been leased to the United States for use as a naval base.

Hawaii's governor placed the islands under martial law. Restrictions applied to everyone.

December 8. The United States declared war on Japan.

December 9. One hundred and sixty Hawaiian *issei* (Japanese immigrants) community leaders were sent to the Sand Island (Honolulu) detention camp.

December 11. Germany and Italy declared war on the United States. In response, the United States declared war on Germany and Italy.

December 15. Secretary of the Navy Frank Knox stated that "the most effective fifth-column secret enemy sympathizers work of the entire war was done in Hawaii," which implicated Japanese Americans as saboteurs. The statement, later found to be based largely on rumors, was false.

December 18. General Delos C. Emmons was named new commander of the U.S. Army and Admiral Chester Nimitz became commander of the U.S. Navy. General Walter C. Short and Admiral Husband E. Kimmel, who had previously occupied the positions, were each cited for "error of judgment" because they had failed to foresee the Japanese attack on Pearl Harbor; they were forced to retire.

December 19. General Delos Emmons rejected a suggestion made by the Joint Chiefs of Staff in Washington to intern (detain) all persons of Japanese ancestry residing in Hawaii at either the former leper colony site on Molokai or in mainland detention camps.

December 24. General John L. DeWitt, head of the Western Defense Command, rejected the idea of interning Japanese Americans by stating, "An American citizen, after all, is an American citizen." He changed his mind the following year.

December 29. Fifty Koreans had registered for training with the California National Guard. A separate Korean guard unit was formed soon after.

1942 It was widely believed that despite the loyalty to America demonstrated by the Japanese Americans, they would assist the Japanese in the event of a Japanese invasion of the West Coast. *(Also see entry dated November, 1941.)*

The first boatload of 172 *issei* (Japanese immigrant) internees departed Honolulu for mainland internment camps. By the end of 1943, a total of 1,037 Japanese would be sent from Hawaii to mainland internment camps.

A Caucasian was convicted of spying for Japan. Between 1942 and 1944, 18 Caucasians were charged with spying for Japan; at least ten were convicted. In contrast, no person of Japanese ancestry was ever charged with espionage.

Captain Joseph J. Rocheford broke the Japanese naval code, which helped the United States win the Battle of Midway. *(Also see entry dated June 4–6, 1942.)*

Under General John L. DeWitt's orders, all persons of Japanese ancestry in the Pacific Coast region were confined in temporary detention camps called "assembly centers." *(Also see entry dated February 20, 1942.)*

The all-*nisei* battalion from Hawaii was sent for training at Camp McCoy, Wisconsin, and on June 12 became the 100th Infantry Battalion. *(Also see entry dated May 26, 1942.)*

January 5. The War Department classified Japanese American men of draft age as 4C, enemy aliens. This designation was not changed until January 1943.

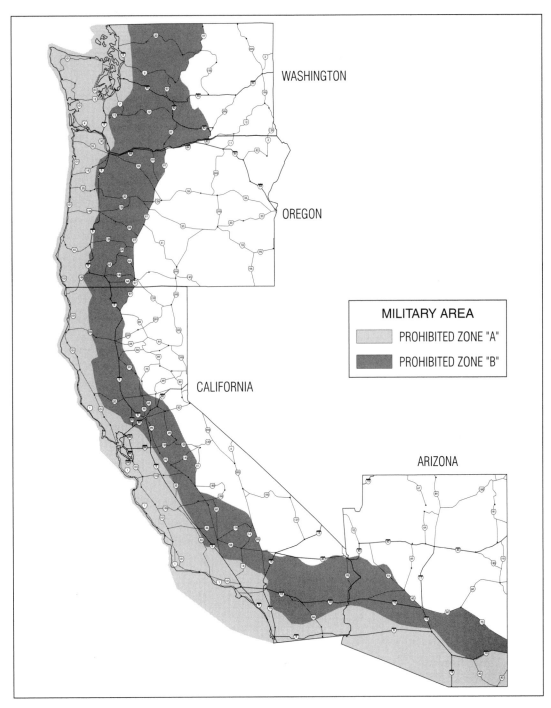

MILITARY AREA

PROHIBITED ZONE "A"

PROHIBITED ZONE "B"

WASHINGTON

OREGON

CALIFORNIA

ARIZONA

Map of California Military Zones

January 25. The Roberts Commission, headed by Supreme Court Justice Owen J. Roberts, issued its investigation report on the attack on Pearl Harbor. Based on rumors and innuendo, the report blamed an alleged espionage network involving Japanese Americans in Hawaii and heightened the fear of possible sabotage on the West Coast.

January 26. Hearst newspapers on the West Coast launched a vilifying attack on Japanese Americans and began the public outcry for a mass exclusion policy.

February 9. General Delos Emmons rejected a War Department order directing him to fire all Japanese American civilians employed by the army in Hawaii.

February 19. President Franklin D. Roosevelt signed Executive Order 9066 authorizing the Secretary of War or his designated military commander to establish military areas and to evacuate civilians from these areas. This action was responsible for forcibly relocating more than 120,000 persons of Japanese ancestry from a zone on the West Coast to internment camps in the West.

February 20. General John L. DeWitt was appointed by the secretary of war to administer Executive Order 9066 as he saw fit. *(Also see entries dated December 24, 1941, and February 19, 1942.)*

February 21. The Tolan Committee (also known as the House of Representatives Select Committee Investigating National Defense Migration) held its first meeting in San Francisco.

February 25. Residents of Japanese ancestry on Terminal Island in Los Angeles Harbor were given 48 hours to leave the island. *(Also see entry dated February 20, 1942.)*

March 1. General John L. DeWitt established the Wartime Civilian Control Administration to handle forced removal of Japanese Americans from their homes and interim detention. Colonel Karl R. Bendetsen was put in charge. *(Also see entry dated February 20, 1942.)*

Ten Relocation Camps

Under the terms of Executive Order 9066, the U.S. government created the ten camps listed below, to house the 120,000 Japanese Americans who were forcibly removed from their homes and incarcerated. *(Also see entry dated February 19, 1942.)* ☉

Camp	State	Date Opened	Date Closed	Internees
Amache Relocation Center	Colorado	August 24, 1942	October 15, 1945	7,318
Gila River Relocation Center	Arizona	July 20, 1942	November 10, 1945	13,348
Heart Mountain Relocation Center	Wyoming	August 12, 1942	November 10, 1945	10,767
Jerome Relocation Center	Arkansas	October 6, 1942	June 30, 1944	8,497
Manzanar Relocation Center	California	March 21, 1942	November 21, 1945	10,046
Minidoka Relocation Center	Idaho	August 10, 1942	October 28, 1945	9,397
Poston Relocation Center	Arizona	May 8, 1942	November 28, 1945	17,814
Rohwer Relocation Center	Arkansas	September 18, 1942	November 30, 1945	8,475
Topaz Relocation Center	Utah	September 1, 1942	October 31, 1945	8,130
Tule Lake Relocation Center	California	May 27, 1942	March 20, 1946	18,789

March 2. General John L. DeWitt, Western Defense commander, issued Public Proclamation No. 1 ordering the removal of persons of Japanese ancestry from Bainbridge Island, Washington. This was the first of 108 military proclamations that resulted in the detention of over 120,000 Japanese Americans from the West Coast in internment camps, or "relocation centers." *(Also see entry dated February 19, 1942.)*

First Filipino Battalion

March 18. President Franklin D. Roosevelt signed Executive Order 9102 establishing the War Relocation Authority to supervise the movement of Japanese American internees. *(Also see entry dated February 19, 1942.)*

March 21. Congress passed Public Law 77–503, making any violation of the military orders under Executive Order 9066 a crime, punishable by a fine of not more than $5,000, imprisonment for up to one year, or both. *(Also see entry dated February 19, 1942.)*

March 28. Attorney Minoru Yasui turned himself in for arrest at the Portland, Oregon, police station to test the discriminatory curfew regulations issued by General John L. DeWitt. *(Also see entry dated February 20, 1942.)*

Edward Laning painting, *Interrogation*. Interrogators were trained at the MIS language school

April 2. The state of California fired all Japanese Americans in the state's civil service.

April 20. At the request of the U.S. government, 141 South American civilians of Japanese ancestry arrived in San Francisco aboard a U.S. vessel. By the end of 1943, 2,100 persons of Japanese ancestry, mostly from Peru, had been taken as hostages for future prisoner exchanges.

April 22. The War Department completed the formation of the First Filipino Infantry Battalion.

May. Gordon Hirabayashi, a student at the University of Washington in Seattle, refused to follow curfew and exclusion (detention) orders in order to test their constitutionality. (*Also see entry dated March 28, 1942.*)

May. Of those sent to detention camps, the average age for *issei* (Japanese immigrant) males was 54 years; for *issei* females it was 47 years. (*Also see entry dated February 19, 1942.*)

May 12. Kanesaburo Oshima was shot and killed by a guard at the Fort Sills, Oklahoma, Internment Camp. *(Also see entry dated February 19, 1942.)*

May 26. An all-*nisei* (children of Japanese immigrants) infantry battalion was formed in Hawaii.

May 30. Fred Korematsu was arrested in Oakland, California, for violating orders to report for detention. He had not accompanied his family when they reported for detention becasue he was planning to marry and move east. *(Also see entry dated February 19, 1942.)*

June 1. The Army Intelligence School, at which soldiers learned Japanese, was moved from San Francisco's Presidio base to Camp Savage, Minnesota, and was reorganized as the Military Intelligence Service (MIS) Language School. Japanese Americans were often used as interrogators during World War II.

June 4–6. The Battle of Midway (a pair of islands 1,304 miles northwest of Hawaii) was fought. It was considered to be the turning point of the war in the Pacific. U.S. Naval Intelligence reported that the Japanese naval fleet was virtually destroyed.

Although the threat of a West Coast invasion, the premise for interning Japanese Americans, no longer existed after the decisive Battle of Midway, the United States continued to detain them. At that time only 17,000 Japanese were in detention camps; 120,000 would eventually be held. *(Also see entry dated February 19, 1942.)*

June 5. Japanese were removed from Military Area No. 1, which included the western halves of Washington, Oregon, and California, and southern Arizona. *(Also see entry dated February 19, 1942.)*

June 17. Milton Eisenhower resigned as director of the War Relocation Authority, the governmental body that provided for the relocation, maintenance, and supervision of Japanese Americans. Eisenhower had stated that he was "sick of the job" and often had trouble sleeping at night. He was succeeded by Dillon S. Myer.

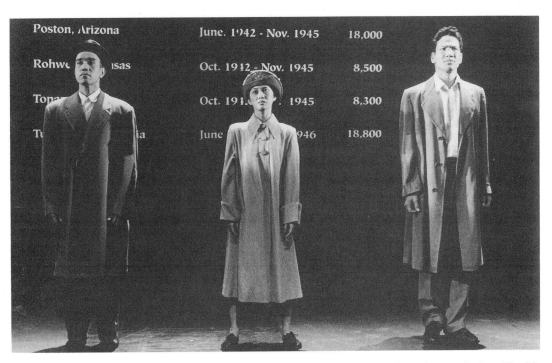

Poston, Arizona	June. 1942 - Nov. 1945	18,000
Rohwe... ...sas	Oct. 1942 - Nov. 1945	8,500
Top...	Oct. 194... ...1945	8,300
T... ...ia	June ... 946	18,800

Ping Chong's play *Deshima* **deals with internment of Japanese Americans during World War II**

June 26. Native Sons of the Golden West, a Chinese civil rights group, filed suit in San Francisco to strip Japanese Americans of their citizenship.

July. Mitsuye Endo filed a writ of *habeas corpus* (an order requiring that a prisoner receive a hearing by a judge so as to prevent illegal detainment) challenging the government's right to detain her. Endo, a young *nisei*, was a Methodist, spoke no Japanese, had never even visited Japan, and had a brother in the U.S. Army. Her case was not resolved for three and a half years, during which time she remained in the Tule Lake (California) Internment Camp. *(Also see entries dated February 19, 1942, and December 18, 1945.)*

July 27. Hirota Isomura and Toshio Obata were shot and killed by guards at the Lordsburg, New Mexico, internment camp. Both victims were invalids, Obata a hospital patient. *(Also see entry dated February 19, 1942.)*

October 30. The army completed its transfer of all Japanese American detainees from 15 temporary assembly centers to 10 permanent War Relocation

Authority detention camps, called relocation centers. *(Also see entry dated February 19, 1942, and chart, p. 69.)*

November 18. The Poston Strike, the first large-scale protest by detainees in internment camps, occurred at the Poston War Relocation Center in Arizona.

December 6. Mass demonstrations erupted at the Manzanar, California, detention camp to protest the arrest without charge of Harry Ueno. James Ito and James Kanagawa were killed when military police fired into a crowd.

1943   The all-*nisei* (children of Japanese immigrants) 100th Battalion was incorporated into the all-Japanese American 442d Regimental Combat Team. They were formally merged in Italy six months later. *(Also see entries dated 1942, May 1943, and June 10, 1944.)*

February. The 100th Infantry Battalion at Camp McCoy, Wisconsin, was ordered to Camp Shelby, Mississippi, to complete training. *(Also see entries dated May 26, 1942, and 1942.)*

February 5. The Wyoming state legislature denied U.S. citizens interned at its Heart Mountain detention camp the right to vote. Similar laws were passed by other detention-camp states. *(Also see entry dated February 19, 1942.)*

February 8. A loyalty questionnaire was administered by the U.S. government at all ten detention camps to men and women over age 17.

One of the purposes of the questionnaire was to identify and register *nisei* men for the draft, but the questions were worded in such a way that Japanese Americans could not help incriminating themselves or renouncing their loyalty to their mother country. No other ethnic group had its loyalty challenged in this way during World War II.

February 14. Japanese Americans interned at Heart Mountain Internment Camp organized to protest the loyalty questionnaire, claiming imprisonment without due process, which conflicts with the constitutional guarantee of fairness in the administration of justice. *(Also see entries dated February 19, 1942, and February 8, 1943.)*

Sample Questions from Loyalty Questionnaire

Question 27 (directed at draft-age males) asked: "Are you willing to serve in the armed forces of the United States on combat duty, wherever ordered?"

Question 28 (directed at all internees) asked: "Will you swear unqualified allegiance to the United States of America and faithfully defend the United States from any or all attack by foreign or domestic sources, and forswear any form of allegiance or obedience to the Japanese emperor, or any other foreign government, power or organization?"

Together, these two questions asked Japanese Americans to make choices that by right they should never have been asked to make. ✪

March 20. The War Relocation Authority was authorized to issue conditional leave permits to those internment camp detainees cleared by Washington; leaves were issued with restrictions. *(Also see entry dated February 19, 1942.)*

April. The War Department insisted on revising General John L. DeWitt's final report in order to conceal evidence that would have been damaging to the government in the pending Yasui and Hirabayashi cases. *(Also see entries dated March 28, 1942, and May 5, 1942.)*

April 9. It was determined by California attorney general Robert W. Kenny that nationals of the United States and citizens of the Philippines were allowed to hold real property in California.

April 11. James Hatsuaki Wakasa, age 63, was shot and killed by a camp guard at the Topaz detention camp in Utah for wandering too close to the fence.

April 13. General John DeWitt testified before the House Naval Affairs Subcommittee in San Francisco: "A Jap's a Jap. You can't change him by giving him a piece of paper."

April 17. U.S. Attorney General Francis Biddle in a memorandum to President Franklin D. Roosevelt stated: "I shall not institute criminal proceedings [against Italian and German aliens] on exclusion orders which seem to me unconstitutional. . . . It [Executive Order 9066] was never intended to apply to Italians and Germans." *(Also see entry dated February 19, 1942.)*

May. The all-Japanese American 442d Regimental Combat Team assembled for training at Camp Shelby, Mississippi.

June 21. The Supreme Court ruled on *Hirabayashi* v. *United States,* declaring that the curfew law imposed on all persons of Japanese ancestry was constitutional. *(Also see entries dated May 1942, and April 1943.)*

June 29. Galley proof of General John L.DeWitt's original Final Report was destroyed and all records on the matter placed in a confidential file. (A galley proof is a version of typeset copy for review before a document is printed.) *(Also see entries dated April 1943 and January 1944.)*

July 15. The War Relocation Authority designated Tule Lake, California, as a segregation center for those detainees who would not sign a loyalty oath. *(Also see entry dated February 8, 1943.)*

September 2. The all-*nisei* 100th Infantry Battalion, which had left Camp Shelby (Mississippi) on August 11th, landed at Oran, North Africa. On September 26, the 100th secured a beachhead landing at Salerno, Italy. *(Also see entry dated 1942.)*

November 4. A mass demonstration took place at Tule Lake internment camp in California to protest the death of a farm worker. The army entered the camp with tanks and continued to occupy it until January 14, 1944. *(Also see entry dated July, 15, 1943.)*

Chinese immigrants were granted the right to naturalization by the U.S. government as a gesture of goodwill toward an ally. (China was a U.S. ally during World War II.)

December 1. Elmer Kira was shot and wounded by a guard at the Gila River, Arizona, detention camp. He was transferred to Arizona State Hospital.

December 4. Military Order No. 45, was issued; it exempted Koreans in the United States from enemy alien status.

December 9. The U.S. Senate passed Joint Resolution 93, granting the Philippines independence by presidential proclamation once the Japanese had been defeated and normal conditions had been restored in the islands.

December 17. Congress passed the so-called Magnuson Act "to repeal the Chinese Exclusion Act, to establish quotas, and for other purposes." This law allowed Chinese to become naturalized citizens and gave China a quota of 105 immigrants per year. *(Also see entry dated 1882.)*

1944   The War Relocation Authority announced that all relocation centers would be closed by the end of 1945. *(Also see entry dated February 19, 1942.)*

January. General John L. DeWitt's Final Report was released by the War Department. Based on false claims, it declared all Japanese "an enemy race."

January 20. The War Department reinstated the draft for *nisei* in detention camps. *(Also see entry dated February 19, 1942.)*

February 16. The War Relocation Authority was transferred to the Department of the Interior.

March 1. The Fair Play Committee was organized at Heart Mountain Internment Camp (Wyoming) to protest the drafting of detainees. The committee held a mass meeting and 400 *nisei* voted unanimously to resist the draft until their constitutional rights were restored. *(Also see entry dated February 19, 1942.)*

March 24. One hundred six *nisei* soldiers at Fort McClellan, Alabama, refused to undergo combat training in protest of their families' continued incarceration. Twenty-one were court-martialed and sentenced to prison terms. Others were assigned to the 1800th General Service Battalion.

May 24. James Okamoto was shot and killed by a guard at California's Tule Lake Internment Camp.

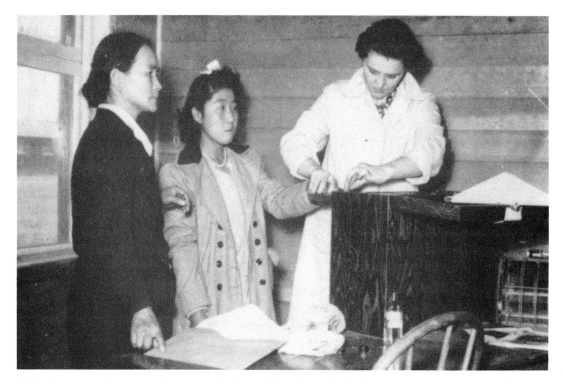

All internees 12 years of age and older at the Tule Lake internment camp were finger-printed and photographed

June 2. The all-Japanese American 442d Regimental Combat Team landed in Italy. It suffered 34 percent casualties and became the most decorated unit of its size and length of service during World War II. *(Also see entry dated May 1943.)*

June 10. The 100th Infantry Battalion and 442d Regimental Combat Team were formally united. By that time the 100th had sustained over 900 casualties and was known as the "Purple Heart Battalion." (The Purple Heart is awarded to soldiers who are wounded in battle.) *(Also see entries dated 1942 and May 1943.)*

June 26. Sixty-three young *nisei* men at Heart Mountain Internment Camp Wyoming were convicted of refusing to report for induction (the draft). Two hundred and sixty-seven men held at detention camps were eventually convicted of draft resistance.

July 1. President Franklin D. Roosevelt signed Public Law No. 405, allowing U.S. citizens to renounce their citizenship in time of war.

August 1. Manuel Luis Quezon y Molina (1878–1944), president of the Commonwealth of the Philippines, died in New York. After the Japanese invasion of the Philippines, he had been removed to the United States.

August 30. Koreans in the continental United States organized the Post-War Assistance Society and began to send relief goods to Korea. Another society with an identical name was established in Hawaii on March 10 and began to collect relief goods to be sent to Korea after the war.

September 7. The Western Defense Command issued Public Proclamation No. 24 revoking exclusion orders and military restrictions against persons of Japanese ancestry.

October 19. Martial law was terminated in Hawaii. *(Also see entry dated December 7, 1941.)*

October 30. The all-Japanese American100th/442d Regimental Combat Team rescued the Texas "Lost Battalion" after five days of continuous battle. The unit suffered over 800 casualties, including 184 dead, to rescue 211 Texans.

November 2. Seven leaders of the Heart Mountain Fair Play Committee were convicted of counseling others to resist the draft. *(Also see entry dated March 1, 1944.)*

December 17. Anticipating the Supreme Court's decision of the following day, the War Department revoked the West Coast exclusion order aimed at Japanese Americans, to be effective January 2, 1945. *(Also see entry dated February 19, 1942.)*

December 18. The Supreme Court ruled on the cases of *Korematsu* v. *United States* and *Endo, Ex parte.* In *Korematsu,* the Court ruled the evacuation order (Executive Order 9066) constitutional. In *Endo,* the same Court contradicted itself by declaring that the government could not hold a loyal, law-abiding citizen in detention against his or her will. *(Also see entries dated February 19, 1942, and July 1942.)*

The 442d Regimental Combat Team, November 1944

1945 The United States War Department set the 38th parallel in Korea as the dividing line between Soviet-occupied North Korea and American-occupied South Korea.

January 2. Japanese Americans forcibly interned were allowed to return to the West Coast as of this date. *(Also see entry dated February 19, 1942.)*

April 5. The supposedly unbreakable Gothic Line in northern Italy was broken by the 100th/442d Regimental Combat Team in the Po Valley Campaign. *(Also see entries dated 1943, May 1943, June 2, 1944, and June 10, 1944.)*

April 29. The 522d Artillery Battalion (of the 442d Regimental Combat Team, temporarily assigned to another unit) was among the first U.S. troops to liberate the Dachau concentration camp in Germany. *(Also see entries dated 1943, May 1943, June 2, 1944, and June 10, 1944.)*

May 7. Germany surrendered to the Allies, ending World War II in Europe.

June. Japan wanted to end the war and sought mediation from the Soviet Union.

August 6. The first atomic bomb used in warfare was dropped on Hiroshima, Japan, by the United States. Sixty percent of the city was wiped out.

August 8. The Soviet Union entered the war against Japan and invaded Manchuria (in northeast China, which was occupied by Japan.)

August 9. The U.S. dropped a second atomic bomb, this time on the seaport of Nagasaki, Japan. An estimated 340,000 persons died from the attacks on Hiroshima and Nagasaki and subsequent effects of exposure to radiation. *(Also see entry dated August 6, 1945.)*

August 14. Japanese Emperor Hirohito broadcast Japan's decision to surrender unconditionally.

September 2. Japan's surrender was formally received by General Douglas MacArthur, Supreme Allied commander, aboard the USS *Missouri* in Tokyo Bay.

December 14. The 10th District Court of Appeals overturned the convictions of the seven Heart Mountain Fair Play Committee leaders. *(Also see entry dated November 2, 1944.)*

December 28. President Harry S Truman signed into law the War Brides Act of 1945, allowing 722 Chinese and 2,042 Japanese women who had married American servicemen to come to the United States between 1946 and 1953. (Women of European descent who had married U.S. servicemen during World War II were also covered by the terms of the War Brides Act.)

1946   Filipino and Indian immigrants gained naturalization privileges in recognition of their support and contributions during World War II.

After World War II, Japanese American athletic leagues were rebuilt, starting with the Nisei Athletic Union in both Northern and Southern California.

January 9. The first Congressional Medal of Honor awarded to a Japanese American was given posthumously to Pfc (private first class) Sadao S. Munemori, who was killed in action on April 5, 1945, in Italy. This honor was bestowed after an investigation by the chair of the Military Affairs Committee found that no *nisei* had been granted the Medal of Honor despite the fact that a substantial number had been recommended for the award.

Ellison Onizuka

February 23. A group of 432 persons of Japanese ancestry—reportedly disloyal citizens—were repatriated to Japan.

March 20. The last of the detention camps, Tule Lake in California, was closed. Many of the Japanese Americans in the camps had nowhere to go, having sold all their possessions during their evacuation. The U.S. government provided them with nothing more than train fare back to where they had lived before being interned. *(Also see entries dated February 19, 1942, and November 4, 1943.)*

June 14. President Harry S Truman signed the Filipino Naturalization Act into law, allowing Filipino immigrants to become naturalized citizens of the United States. *(Also see entries dated 1906, February 26, 1930, and March 24, 1934)*

June 24. Ellison Onizuka, the first Asian American astronaut, was born in Kealakekua on the Kona coast of Hawaii.

Onizuka dreamed of imaginary spacecraft as a child and knew he wanted to be an astronaut by the time he was a teenager. After becoming a member of the Air Force Reserve Officer Training Corps at the University of Colorado, he went on to enter active duty with the U.S. Air Force in 1970. There he became an aerospace flight test engineer.

Onizuka eventually became a colonel and flight instructor at Edwards Air Force Base and began astronaut training in 1978. In 1985 he was part of the crew of the space shuttle *Discovery* mission, the first Hawaiian, first Japanese American, and first Buddhist to orbit in space. In 1986, on his second space shuttle mission, he perished in the explosion of the *Challenger* along with the other six crew members.

June 29. Congress approved the G.I. Fiancées Act, which enabled women or men engaged to U.S. military personnel to immigrate to the United States. Immigrants from Japan were allowed for the first time since 1924.

June 30. The War Relocation Authority program was officially ended. *(Also see entry dated March 18, 1942.)*

July 2. The Luce-Celler Bill was signed into law, allowing Asian Indians to become U.S. citizens and establishing a quota of 100 immigrants from India to the United States per year.

July 4. The Philippines gained independence from the United States. This had been promised in 1934 when the Tydings-McDuffie Act was passed. *(Also see entry dated March 24, 1934.)*

July 15. The all-Japanese-military unit, the 100th Battalion/442d Regimental Combat Team, paraded down Constitution Avenue in Washington, D.C., and received a Presidential Unit Citation (their seventh) from President Harry S Truman. *(Also see entry dated April 5, 1945.)*

August 20. Connie Chung, the first Asian American and second woman to become a nightly news anchor at a major television network, was born in suburban Washington, D.C.

Chung's career began at a local television station in Washington, D.C., and by 1971 she had worked her way up to CBS's Washington bureau, covering stories of national importance and traveling with President Richard M. Nixon. She went on to a distinguished career in broadcast journalism at CBS and NBC, where she had her first taste of anchoring the network evening news, sitting in for Tom Brokaw. She later became a co-anchor with Dan Rather of the CBS Evening News. Chung was the first Asian American journalist to achieve national network anchor status. Although she was a celebrity and role model, winning three national Emmy awards and a Peabody, in May 1995, CBS relieved Chung of her duties.

In July 1995, Chung and her husband, talk show host Maury Povich, adopted a baby boy, Matthew Jay Povich. The adoption was finalized just four days after her dismissal by CBS News.

Connie Chung

October 13. Dale Minami, attorney and activist, was born in Los Angeles, California.

Minami earned his law degree from the University of California at Berkeley School of Law and went on to become a cofounder in 1972 of the Asian Law Caucus and its first lawyer. He also became a cofounder of the Asian American Bar Association of the Greater Bay Area and the Asian Pacific Bar of California, a statewide consortium of bar associations. In 1989, Minami cofounded the Coalition of Asian Pacific Americans. He would eventually set up a private law practice in San Francisco. Minami has received many awards for his service to the Asian American community.

1947 Chinese in the United States sent $70 million to their families, relatives, and to organizations in China between 1938 and 1947. The country was devastated by the end of World War II, after being invaded by Japan and at the same time experiencing a major civil war between the Nationalists (under Chiang Kai-shek) and the Communists (under Mao Zedong).

December 23. President Harry S Truman granted full pardons to the 267 Japanese American draft resisters who had violated the Selective Training and Service Act of 1940. *(Also see entry dated June 26, 1944.)*

1948 At the London Olympics, Filipino American Vicki Manolo Draves became the first woman in Olympic history to win both the high (platform) and low (springboard) diving Gold Medals. Another diver, Korean American Major Sammy Lee, won the Gold Medal in the men's diving division. He would later win another Gold Medal at the 1952 Helsinki Games in Finland. Japanese American Harold Sakata, a native Hawaiian, won the Silver Medal in weightlifting. *(Also see entry dated 1952.)*

Dale Minami

January 19. In *The People* v. *Oyama*, the Supreme Court ruled California's escheat action—in which the state had attempted to seize lands belonging to Japanese Americans—unconstitutional.

May 3. In *Shelley* v. *Kraemer*, the Supreme Court ruled that race-restrictive housing covenants (agreements) were unenforceable. Members of minority groups would continue to face discrimination in finding housing, but this case affirmed that landlords and real estate agents could not use race as a reason not to rent or sell to a prospective client. Discrimination based on race in housing remains illegal.

June 7. The Supreme Court invalidated racial restrictions of commercial fishing licenses in *Takahashi* v. *California Fish and Game Commission;* it declared Section 990 of the Fish and Game Code of California unconstitutional. Section 990 had denied commercial fishing licenses to Japanese Americans.

At the 1948 Olympics, Vicki Manolo Draves (center) won gold medals in the platform and springboard diving competitions

June 25. President Harry S Truman signed into law the Displaced Persons Act of 1948, granting legal immigrant status to as many as 15,000 Chinese stranded in the United States after the Communist victory in China. The Communists, under the leadership of Mao Zedong, had waged a civil war with the Nationalists, who were led by Chiang Kai-shek and supported by the United States and Great Britain. The Nationalists steadily lost ground throughout 1948 and 1949. *(Also see entries dated 1936, October 1, 1949, and October 8, 1949.)*

July 2. President Harry S Truman signed into law the Japanese American Evacuation Claims Act, enabling Japanese Americans who had been interned to file claims against the government for their financial losses. Unfortunately,

South Korean president Syngman Rhee

claimants received less than ten cents on the dollar for lost property. Even worse, many were not even able to file a claim because required documentation had been lost or destroyed during the internment. *(Also see entry dated February 19, 1942.)*

August 14. The new Republic of Korea (the South) was inaugurated at a ceremony in Seoul, Korea, with Syngman Rhee as its founder and first president. *(Also see entries dated 1904 and 1945.)*

October 6. The Supreme Court declared California's ban on interracial marriage unconstitutional.

1949 **October 1.** In China, the Communists, with Mao Zedong as Chairman, proclaimed the People's Republic of China and established the capital at Beijing.

Asian American Population in 1950

Population category	Number
Total U.S. population	151,325,798
Total Asian American population	599,091
Chinese	150,005
Filipino (from the Philippines)	122,707
Japanese	326,379
Korean	7,030

Source: U.S. Bureau of Census, Decennial Censuses of Population

October 7. Iva Toguri D'Aquino (1916–), a Japanese American radio announcer also known as Tokyo Rose, was sentenced to a ten-year prison term in San Francisco. She was convicted as a traitor for disseminating propaganda, including continual announcements that the Japanese were winning World War II, on the Japanese Broadcasting Corporation radio station. She was released on January 28, 1956. (Propaganda is selected information, true or false, promoted with the aim of persuading people to adopt a particular belief, attitude, or course of action.)

October 8. The Nationalists in China, who had tried to resist the Communist takeover there, were expelled from the mainland by Communist forces. Led by General Chiang Kai-shek, the government of the Republic of China was officially transferred to Taiwan, on the island of Formosa. By early 1950, all Nationalists had been driven from the mainland and had taken refuge in Taiwan.

1950

June 25. The Korean War began when the Soviet-armed North Koreans invaded the southern Republic of Korea. (North Korea had become a Communist state in 1946 with the establishment of the Kim Il Sung regime.) *(Also see entries dated 1945 and August 14, 1948.)*

June 27. United States forces joined United Nations troops on the side of the Republic of Korea (known as South Korea) at the order of President Harry S Truman. During their tours of duty, some U.S. servicemen married Korean women. These "war brides" returned with their husbands to the United States when the Korean War ended in stalemate in 1953. (Neither South Korea nor North Korea, which was eventually aided by the Chinese, was able to gain significant ground

Iva Toguri D'Aquino (Tokyo Rose) talks with her attorney, Wayne Collins

after Chinese forces helped push U.S. and South Korean soldiers back into South Korea. An armistice ended the war on July 23. Korea remains divided.) The Korean War brought tremendous destruction and casualties to both North and South Korea. Following the war, many Korean war orphans were adopted by U.S. citizens. *(Also see entries dated 1945 and August 14, 1948.)*

August. General Douglas MacArthur, commanding general of the United Nations forces in Korea, made plans to assign 20,000 to 30,000 Korean Army recruits to U.S. Army units during the Korean War. This was known as the Korean Augmentation to U.S. Army Program.

September 23. The McCarran Internal Security Act was passed by Congress over President Harry S Truman's veto. The act called for the registration of

Communists and Communist organizations. Its Title II provision, citing the incarceration of Japanese Americans as a precedent, authorized the president to incarcerate any person (Chinese Communists were particular targets) on mere suspicion—without evidence. Six sites for detention camps in the United States were designated, one of which was Tule Lake, California, the location of a former Japanese American internment camp. *(Also see entry dated February 19, 1942.)*

1951 The Communist government in China strengthened its control. Chinese in the United States were prevented from sending money to their families and relatives in mainland China.

The MGM movie, *Go For Broke,* based on the all-Japanese American 100th/442nd Regimental Combat Team, was released. *(Also see entry dated June 10, 1944.)*

Wang Laboratories, maker of computer components, was founded by An Wang. Wang's goal was to create small-scale commercial uses for the magnetic core memory (a component of early computers) device that he had invented. Wang Laboratories would grow into one of the most successful businesses in American history, and Wang himself was estimated by *Forbes* magazine in 1984 to be the fifth-richest person in America.

April 11. General Douglas MacArthur was relieved of his command in the Far East by President Harry S Truman. He was succeeded by General Matthew B. Ridgway. Truman fired MacArthur over disagreements on how to conduct the Korean War. (MacArthur wanted to attack China, which had come into the war on the side of North Korea.)

September. Japan and 55 other nations signed the San Francisco Peace Treaty. This treaty officially ended the state of war that existed between the Western powers (primarily America and Great Britain) and Japan and restored Japan as an independent nation. U.S. occupation of Japan ended in April 1952 when the treaty went into effect. On the same day, Japan signed a security treaty with the United States that continued the maintenance of U.S. military bases in Japan and committed the United States to defend Japan.

1952 At the Summer Olympics in Helsinki, Finland, Ford Konno and Yoshinbu Oyakawa became the first Japanese Americans to win Olympic Gold Medals in

Gold medalist Tommy Kono set a new 1952 Olympic record in the weightlifting event

swimming; Japanese American Tommy Kono won the Gold for weightlifting; and Korean American Sammy Lee set new records when he won his second Gold Medal for diving. Lee's achievement came on August 1, 1952, his thirty-second birthday. *(Also see entry dated 1948.)*

The McCarran-Walter Immigration and Nationality Act went into effect, repealing the National Origins Act of 1924 and allowing immigration quotas from Japan and other Asian countries. The McCarran-Walter Act (Immigration and Nationality Act of 1952) was passed by Congress over President Harry S Truman's veto. The act conferred the rights of naturalization and eventual citizenship on Asians not born in the United States and set a quota of 105 immigrants per year from each Asian country. *(Also see entry dated May 26, 1924.)*

April. The U.S.-Japan peace treaty, signed in September 1951, went into effect. The treaty formally ended war between the two nations, although there had been no actual armed conflict since 1944. *(Also see entry dated September 1951.)*

April 17. In its ruling on *Fujii* v. *California*, the California Supreme Court found that alien land laws violated the Fourteenth Amendment by being racially discriminatory. The Fourteenth Amendment holds that "all persons born or naturalized in the United States . . . are citizens of the United States. . . . No state shall make or enforce any law which shall abridge the privileges . . . of citizens of the United States. . . . nor deny to any person . . . the equal protection of the laws." *(Also see entry dated May 19, 1913.)*

1953

The Refugee Relief Act, set to expire at the end of 1956, allowed Chinese political refugees to come to the United States.

The martial art of judo (a system of bare–handed fighting designed to reduce the risk of injury to the participants) was formally recognized as a sport by the Amateur Athletic Union (AAU) due to the efforts of *nisei* Yosh Uchida of San Jose State University.

May 2. The day was declared Korean Day in the United States, and U.S. citizens were encouraged to make donations in money and materials to assist the war-beleaguered Koreans.

July 23. The armistice ending the Korean War was signed. *(Also see entry dated June 27, 1950.)*

September 25. California Governor Earl Warren appointed John F. Aiso of Los Angeles a judge. He was the first judge of *nisei* origin in the continental United States.

1954

The All-American Overseas Chinese Anti-Communist League was established in New York to assure Americans that the Chinese living among them were not communists.

Japanese American Sergeant Hiroshi Miyamura, a veteran of the 442d Regimental Combat Team during World War II, received the Congressional Medal of Honor from President Dwight D. Eisenhower for his actions in the Korean War. *(Also see entry dated May 1943.)*

Patsy Takemoto Mink, a young Japanese American lawyer, was elected president of the Young Democrats political group in Hawaii. *(Also see entry dated 1964.)*

Vietnamese forces defeated the French to regain Vietnam's independence in the battle of Dien Bien Phu. Vietnam had been a French colony since the late nineteenth century.

Hiroshi Miyamura

The Geneva Agreements formulated at the end of the French-Indochinese war provided for a partitioning (division) of Vietnam at the seventeenth parallel until an all-Vietnamese election could be held in 1956. The government in the South was supported by the United States; the North was backed by Communist China and the Soviet Union. (Indochina is a political term for peninsular Southeast Asia between China and India; it now refers to the nations of Vietnam, Laos, and Kampuchea [Cambodia].)

Peruvians of Japanese ancestry who had been held as hostages in U.S. detention camps were allowed to apply for permanent residence status in the United States after Peru refused them reentry. Attorney Wayne M. Collins of San Francisco was instrumental in this effort. *(Also see entry dated April 20, 1942.)*

May 31. The U.S. Supreme Court declared segregated schools unconstitutional. The Court ruled that individual states must end racial segregation in public schools within a "reasonable" time. Although this ruling related specifically to the segregation of African American students, a ruling outlawing racial discrimination supported equal opportunity for other minorities as well.

1955 Chinese American James Wong Howe won an Oscar for cinematography for his work on the film *The Rose Tattoo*. In a career that spanned over fifty years, Howe filmed more than 125 movies, including *The Thin Man*. In 1963 he won a second Academy Award for *Hud*, starring Paul Newman.

Dalip Singh Saund

Filipino Americans were the second-fastest growing ethnic group in the United States. Many Filipino soldiers who had fought in World War II had become citizens. Other new immigrants were war brides and children of Filipino soldiers. The average income of Filipino Americans at that time, however, was very low.

1956 Dalip Singh Saund, an Asian Indian American, won election to the U.S. House of Representatives from the twenty-ninth district of California, becoming the first member of the U.S. House of Representatives of Asian descent.

Harry Holt, a resident of Creswell, Oregon, returned from Korea with eight Korean orphans, whom he adopted. He later established the Holt Adoption Agency, which brought thousands of Korean orphans to the United States.

California alien land laws were repealed by a two-to-one majority by the voters of California. *(Also see entry dated April 17, 1920.)*

1957 Chen-Ning Yang (1922–) and Tsung-dao Lee (1926–) shared the Nobel Prize in physics. The Columbia University Physics Department hailed their "achievement in disputing the accepted principle of the conservation of parity," a long-held tenet of physical law dealing with the movement and behavior of subatomic particles as they split apart upon impact. The discovery was called the "most important development in physics in the last ten years."

Chien-Shiung Wu, a Chinese physicist, collaborated with Yang and Lee (see entry above) on their Nobel Prize-winning physics research.

She would later receive an endowed professorship at Columbia University, followed by several firsts: she was the first woman to receive the Comstock Award from the National Academy of Sciences, the first woman to receive the Research Corporation Award, the first woman to become president of the American Physical Society, the first woman to receive an honorary doctorate of science degree from Princeton University, and the first living scientist to have an asteroid named after her.

Chin-Yang (C.Y.) Lee published the best-selling *Flower Drum Song,* which would provide the basis for the highly successful Rodgers and Hammerstein musical of the same name on Broadway.

Japanese American actor Sessue Hayakawa (1889–1973) starred in *The Bridge on the River Kwai.* He was later nominated for an Academy Award for best supporting actor for his work in the picture.

May 1. The Korean Foundation was organized, with Kim Ho as its president, to promote higher education among Koreans in the United States.

Chien-Shiung Wu

1959 Hiram Fong became the first Chinese American elected to the U.S. Senate, and Daniel Inouye became the first Japanese American elected to the House of Representatives; both were from Hawaii. *(Also see entries dated September 7, 1924, and October 1, 1907.)*

The Immigration and Naturalization Service established a procedure to monitor illegal Chinese immigrants, which resulted in 8,000 confessions of illegal presence in the United States.

Wilfred C. Tsukiyama became the first chief justice of Hawaii's Supreme Court.

Hiram Fong

January 3. President Dwight Eisenhower proclaimed Alaska as the 49th state of the union.

August 21. President Dwight Eisenhower proclaimed Hawaii as the 50th state.

1960 Chinese American sociologist Rose Hum Lee published her study *The Chinese in the United States of America*, an examination of the social structure and assimilation (adapting to customs) of Chinese Americans.

Lee was the first Chinese American woman to head a sociology department at an American university, the University of Chicago, beginning in 1956.

The National Liberation Front, also known as the Vietcong (South Vietnamese Communists), was formed in South Vietnam.

Asian American Population in 1960

Population category	Number
Total U.S. population	179,323,175
Total Asian American population	877,932
Chinese	237,292
Filipino (from the Philippines)	176,310
Japanese	464,332
Korean	no data

Source: U.S. Bureau of Census, Decennial Censuses of Population

1961   William Shao Chang Chen, who would become the first Chinese American major general in the U.S. Armed Forces, graduated from the Army Reserve Officer Training Corps (ROTC) and began a thirty-year career in the U.S. Army.

1962   Daniel K. Inouye was elected U.S. senator from Hawaii. *(Also see entry dated September 7, 1924.)*

President John F. Kennedy signed a presidential directive allowing more than 15,000 refugees from Communist China to enter the United States over a three-year period. Things had been improving for Chinese immigrants since World War II, when China, fighting for the Japanese invaders, became a staunch ally of the United States. Several Refugee Acts before Kennedy's had benefited Chinese immigrants. Kennedy expressed the new attitude, stating that U.S. immigration must be both fair

Daniel K. Inouye

Architect Minoru Yamasaki

and generous. "It it time to correct the mistakes of the past and work toward a better future for all humanity," the president told Congress.

"Spark" Masayaki Matsunaga was elected to the U.S. House of Representatives from Hawaii, where he served seven terms before being elected to the U.S. Senate. *(Also see entry dated October 8, 1916.)*

Seiji Horiuchi of Brighton, Colorado, became the first Japanese American elected to a state legislature in the continental United States.

At age 26, Asian Indian American Zubin Mehta became music director of the Los Angeles Philharmonic Orchestra. He was the youngest conductor of a major American orchestra. *(Also see entry dated 1936.)*

Mehta later became the music director for life of the Israel Philharmonic Orchestra and a leader in the classical music world.

Civil Rights Movement

Civil rights are the rights people have as members of a particular society. Civil rights to which Americans are entitled include the freedoms of speech, religion, and the press, and the rights to own property and to receive equal treatment by the government and by other members of society.

The term "civil rights movement" is used to refer to actions and trends that began in the 1950s, but which peaked during the 1960s and 1970s, when African Americans in particular, along with other minority groups and those sympathetic to their cause, publicly demonstrated to win fair and equal treatment in society. The civil rights movement sought equality for minorities in public education at all levels, in housing, in elections, and in employment.

The Civil Rights Act of 1964 and other legislation and court rulings made discrimination based on race or ethnicity illegal. Although racism and discrimination still exist, neither the government nor any individual can legally discriminate against a member of a racial or ethnic minority.

Mass demonstrations and public confrontations forced schools, public facilities, and government officials to face their long-standing practices of discrimination, and to take action to correct them. ✪

The architectural firm of Yamasaki Associates, headed by Japanese American Minoru Yamasaki, received the commission to design the twin towers of the World Trade Center in New York City. It would be fourteen years before the buildings were complete. When completed, the matching skyscrapers were the tallest buildings in the world.

1963   **August 28**. Thirty-five members of the Japanese American Citizens League participated in the civil rights march on Washington, D.C. The JACL was the only known Asian American organization represented in this group of 200,000 demonstrators for jobs, freedom, peace, and justice for all Americans regardless of race or ethnic background. *(Also see entry dated April 1929.)*

1964   Democrat Patsy Takemoto Mink was elected to Congress. Born in 1927 on the island of Maui in Hawaii, Patsy Takemoto Mink wanted to become a doctor but was rejected by every medical school she applied to. After graduating from the

Yoichi R. Okamoto with President Lyndon B. Johnson

University of Nebraska, she entered the law school at the University of Chicago and eventually started her own law practice in Hawaii. *(Also see entry dated 1954.)*

Yoichi R. Okamoto, a Japanese American, became head of the White House Photo Office for President Lyndon B. Johnson. He remained in that post until 1968.

Okamoto pioneered the use of dramatic, candid photography in the White House as he captured Johnson during the high and low points of his presidency. He had almost unlimited access to the president, a first for a White House photographer. Okamoto's style became the standard for political photographers to follow.

Chinese American author Bette Bao Lord published *Eighth Moon: The True Story of a Young Girl's Life in Communist China,* which recounted the experiences of her sister, Sansan.

Bao's father, an electrical engineer and former colonel in the Nationalist army in China, was sent after World War II to the United States by the Nationalist government. He brought his wife and two of his three young daughters, but the youngest girl, Sansan, was left behind with relatives because her parents felt the long ocean voyage would be too difficult for the infant. They planned to have her come to the United States later, or to return to her soon in China. However, shortly after the family left, the long and bloody civil war in China erupted. When Mao Zedong's Communist Party emerged victorious, Bao Lord's father could not return to China without being prosecuted as a traitor, since he had been a colonel in the Nationalist army. The family could remain in the United States, but they knew that it would be difficult or impossible to get Sansan out of China.

It was not until 1962 that Bao Lord's mother acted out an elaborate plan in which she pretended to be terminally ill in an effort to get the Chinese authorities to allow her youngest daughter to visit her in Hong Kong. Sansan was allowed to visit her mother, after which they both fled to the United States.

Congress passed the Civil Rights Act, outlawing racial discrimination. However, as Attorney General Robert Kennedy told Congress, "Everywhere else in our national life, we have eliminated discrimination based on national origins. Yet this system is still the foundation of our immigration law." The following year, Congress considered immigration reform. *(Also see entry dated October 3, 1965.)*

August. The American destroyer *Maddox* was shelled by the North Vietnamese in the Gulf of Tonkin (an arm of the South China Sea east of North Vietnam.)

August 7. In the Tonkin Gulf Resolution, Congress formally authorized President Lyndon B. Johnson to take military action against North Vietnam.

1965   Rapid population growth, the growth of urban centers, and the increasingly authoritarian (dictatorial) character of the Korean government fueled Korean immigration to the United States. By 1976, Korean immigration had exceeded 30,000, leading to the emergence of "Koreatowns" in Los Angeles and Chicago.

The Filipino American Political Association was established in San Francisco.

The East West Players, the first Asian American theater company in the United States, was founded by a young group of Asian American actors under the leadership of Japanese American Mako. In 1994 Mako would be honored with a star on the Hollywood Walk of Fame.

January. Patsy Takemoto Mink took the oath of office for the first of six consecutive terms as Hawaii's representative to the U.S. Congress. She was the first woman to represent Hawaii, and the first Asian American woman elected to Congress. *(Also see entry dated 1964.)*

October 3. President Lyndon B. Johnson signed a new immigration law that not only repealed the National Origins Act of 1924, but also established a new immigration policy that would enable large numbers of Asian immigrants to come to the United States. The law provided for the annual admission of 170,000 from the Eastern Hemisphere (20,000 per country) and 120,000 from the Western Hemisphere. Immediate family members of U.S. citizens were exempted from these quotas. *(Also see entry dated May 26, 1924.)*

1966   Chinese American Gerald Tsai started the Manhattan Fund, an investment management firm, riding the tide of high-profit years on Wall Street.

March Fong Eu, of Chinese ancestry, was elected to the California legislature, becoming the first Asian American assemblywoman in California history.

Japanese American actor Mako earned an Academy Award nomination for best supporting actor for his work in *The Sand Pebbles*. He won a Golden Globe Award for the performance as well. *(Also see entry dated 1965.)*

1967   Japanese American boxer Paul Fujii won the junior-welterweight boxing championship.

June. Anti-miscegenation laws (prohibiting marriage between members of different races) were ruled unconstitutional by the U.S. Supreme Court in the case *Loving* v. *Virginia*.

President Lyndon B. Johnson signing new immigration law, October 3, 1965

1968   Asian Indian American Har Gobind Khorana (1922–) was awarded the Nobel Prize in physiology for his work in deciphering the genetic code and its role in controlling protein synthesis.

New York City's Whitney Museum of American Art staged a retrospective of the work of Isamu Noguchi, sculptor and architect. *(Also see entry dated 1904.)*

Duke Kahanamoku, Native Hawaiian Olympic swimmer and world-class surfer, died at the age of 77. *(Also see entry dated 1924.)*

Senator Daniel K. Inouye of Hawaii, in his keynote address at the Democratic National Convention in Chicago, established himself as a crusader for social equality as he pleaded for racial understanding. *(Also see entry dated September 7, 1924.)*

103

Professional football player, Roman Gabriel

November 6. Student demonstrations for the establishment of ethnic studies programs began at San Francisco State University and spilled over to the University of California, Berkeley, in 1969.

The Asian American Political Alliance was formed, with chapters at both universities, and began to promote the use of the term "Asian" in place of "Oriental," effectively starting the Asian American movement.

1969 Filipino American Roman Gabriel, professional football player with the Los Angeles Rams, won the Jim Thorpe Trophy, the National Football League's Most Valuable Player Award, given by the Associated Press. Quarterback Gabriel completed 196 of 371 passes that year for 2,779 yards, and set a Rams record with 25 touchdown passes.

As a result of student protests at San Francisco State University and the University of California, Berkeley, Asian American studies programs were established at American universities. Japanese American history was taught as an academic subject for the first time. *(Also see entry dated November 6, 1968.)*

Reflecting the movement for equal rights, Chinese for Affirmative Action (CAA) was founded in San Francisco. CAA was established to assist Asian Americans in their fight for equal employment opportunities. CAA worked with government agencies to develop bilingual (dual language) materials for Asian American job applicants, and developed a counseling program on workers' rights. CAA provides consulting services to employers seeking to fulfill affirmative action employment goals. (Affirmative action is any program or policy designed to increase the numbers of minority group members or of women in jobs or schools from which they were previously wholly or partly excluded.)

Harry Kitano

Sociologist and professor Harry Kitano published *Japanese Americans,* the first comprehensive account of the experiences of Japanese Americans after World War II.

Florence Makita Hongo brought together a dozen Japanese American educators in California to establish what would become the Japanese American Curriculum Project, the nation's largest nonprofit clearinghouse (a central agency for the collection, classification, and distribution of information) for Asian American books and educational materials. In 1994, the group changed its name to the Asian American Curriculum Project.

The first pilgrimages to the former internment campsites of Tule Lake and Manzanar, both in California, began. Other sites would be visited in later years.

Asian American Population in 1970

Population category	Number
Total U.S. population	203,211,926
Total Asian American population	1,429,562
Chinese	436,062
Filipino (from the Philippines)	343,060
Japanese	591,290
Korean	69,150

Source: U.S. Bureau of Census, Decennial Censuses of Population

The annual Manzanar pilgrimage became the most consistent. *(Also see entry dated February 19, 1942.)*

Yoko Ono married musician and ex-Beatle John Lennon. Ono, an avant-garde (experimental) artist and film-maker, eventually collaborated with Lennon on many of his compositions, including the classic song "Imagine."

1970 The Japanese American Citizens League's (JACL) national convention, held in Chicago, passed the first of numerous resolutions seeking redress (reparations) for the internment of Japanese Americans during World War II. The resolution was passed, but little was done to act upon it. Redress became JACL's priority issue in the following years. *(Also see entries dated April 1929, and February 19, 1942.)*

Japanese American employees of the State of California received retirement credit for time spent in

Yoko Ono

detention camps. Eventually, similar credits would be allowed for federal employees and those receiving Social Security. *(Also see entry dated February 19, 1942.)*

Seiji Ozawa was made artistic director of the Tanglewood Music Festival in Massachusetts, the world-renowned summer home of the Boston Symphony Orchestra. *(Also see entry dated 1935.)*

Filipino American José Aruego wrote and illustrated *Juan and the Asuangs: A Tale of Philippine Ghosts and Spirits*, which was named an outstanding picture book of the year by the *New York Times*.

1971 Norman Mineta was elected mayor of San Jose, California, becoming the first Japanese American mayor of a major city. *(Also see entry dated November 12, 1932.)*

Robert Matsui, third generation Japanese American, won his first political campaign when he was elected to the Sacramento, California, City Council, where he served until his successful run for the U.S. Congress in 1978.

Title II of the McCarran Internal Security Act of 1950, which would have legalized detention camps during times of national emergency, was repealed. *(Also see entry dated September 23, 1950.)*

Twelve hundred Vietnam War protesters were awarded $10,000 per individual after being arrested on the Capitol steps and detained for up to 72 hours without being charged with a crime.

Robert Matsui

President Richard M. Nixon appointed Judge Herbert Choy, a Korean American, to the U.S. Court of Appeals for the Ninth Circuit. Choy thus became the first Asian American to be named to a federal court.

Samoan American diver Greg Louganis scored a perfect ten in the Amateur Athletic Union (AAU) Junior Olympics. Louganis went on to become a Gold Medalist in the 1984 and 1988 Olympics. *(Also see entries dated 1984 and 1988.)*

Huynh Cong "Nick" Ut

1972 Ken Kawaichi and Dale Minami cofounded the Asian Law Caucus (ALC), a legal advocacy organization dedicated to helping Asian Americans in the areas of civil rights, employment and housing discrimination, and immigration. Minami became the ALC's first attorney. *(Also see entry dated October 13, 1946.)*

The declaration of martial law in the Philippines increased political activism among Filipino Americans.

Huynh Cong "Nick" Ut won the Pulitzer Prize for photography for his photo of a young, naked Vietnamese girl fleeing her home after being hit by napalm (highly explosive jelled gasoline).

Frank Chin became the first Asian American playwright to have a play produced on a New York stage—*The Chickencoop Chinaman* at the American Place Theatre.

May 10. The Ryukyu Islands, including Okinawa (the scene of severe fighting between Japanese and American troops in 1945), were restored to Japan, ending the United States' twenty-seven-year occupation.

Writer Jeanne Wakatsuki Houston

1973   Seiji Ozawa became music director of the Boston Symphony Orchestra, and thus the first Asian music director of a major American symphony. *(Also see entries dated 1935 and 1970.)*

The Manzanar detention camp was designated a California state historical landmark, with a bronze plaque installed to commemorate the site. In subsequent years, many other internment campsites were awarded similar designations and plaques. *(Also see entry dated February 19, 1942.)*

Japanese American writer Jeanne Wakatsuki Houston, with her husband James Houston, published *Farewell to Manzanar,* a recollection of the Wakatsuki family's memories of three and a half years of internment during World War II. This work is included on many reading lists for young people involved in the study of America's multicultural history. *(Also see entry dated February 19, 1942.)*

109

George Morikami, a former indentured worker at the Yamato (farming) Colony in Boca Raton, Florida, donated 35 acres to Palm Beach County (Florida) for the establishment of a park. (Indentured workers were bound to labor for a stated period; they often agreed to this in exchange for passage from their homelands to the United States.) Morikami Park was dedicated the following year. *(Also see entry dated 1904.)*

Senator Daniel K. Inouye was named to sit on the Senate Select Committee on Presidential Campaign Activities, otherwise known as the Senate Watergate Committee, which investigated wrongdoing in Richard M. Nixon's 1972 presidential campaign. *(Also see September 7, 1924.)*

George Morikami

Under the leadership of K. L. Wang, Chinese Americans established the Organization of Chinese Americans to educate the public on cultural and civil rights issues concerning Chinese Americans. Their inaugural ball was held in June in Washington, D.C.

July 20. Chinese American actor and martial artist Bruce Lee died mysteriously at the age of 32. *(Also see entry dated November 27, 1940.)*

1974   March Fong Eu was elected secretary of state in California with a record-setting three million votes. Eu was reelected four times; in 1994, while serving her fifth term, she was appointed by President Bill Clinton to the post of ambassador to Micronesia. *(Also see entry dated 1966.)*

In *Lau* v. *Nichols*, the Supreme Court ruled that failure to provide adequate education for non-English-speaking students violated the Equal Protection Clause of the Constitution. This decision led to the implementation of classes in and special tutors for English as a second language (ESL) for students of any ethnic background attending public schools.

Norman Y. Mineta of California became the first Japanese American from the continental United States elected to Congress. *(Also see entry dated November 12, 1932.)*

George R. Ariyoshi of Hawaii became the first Japanese American elected governor in the United States.

March Fong Eu

1975 Shahir Kadir, an Indonesian entrepreneur, successfully challenged a discriminatory District of Columbia law limiting business ownership to U.S. citizens.

Ann Kiyomura, a Japanese American, and Kazuko Sawamatsu of Japan won the Wimbledon women's doubles tennis title.

E.O. 9066, Inc. of Los Angeles and the Seattle Redress Committee became the first groups to activate a redress (reparations) campaign on behalf of Japanese Americans who had been imprisoned in internment camps during World War II. *(Also see entry dated February 19, 1942.)*

Emperor Hirohito of Japan made his first post-World War II visit to the United States.

Chinese American author Laurence Yep published *Dragonwings*, the story of a real-life Chinese American aviator who built and flew a flying machine at the beginning of the twentieth century. The book was chosen as a 1976 Newbery Honor Book and received numerous other awards. Yep later adapted his work for the stage, and *Dragonwings* was produced at Lincoln Center in New York and the Kennedy Center in Washington, D.C.

April 15. The Interagency Task Force was created to coordinate all U.S. government activities in evacuating U.S. citizens as well as selected Vietnamese from Vietnam.

Daniel K. Akaka

April 30. South Vietnam surrendered to the Communist forces of the North. The fall of Vietnam and neighboring Cambodia caused large-scale immigration of Vietnamese, Laotian, and Cambodian refugees to the United States. The first-wave refugees came mainly from urban areas, especially Saigon (a former capital of South Vietnam). Later, repression within Vietnam and Laos resulted in a second wave of refugees, called "boat people," who fled their homes to seek immigration to the United States.

May 24. The Indochina Migration and Refugee Assistance Act was passed. The act provided federal funds to reimburse state governments for the expenses of state resettlement programs for Vietnamese and other refugees.

1976   "Spark" Masayuki Matsunaga was elected to the U.S. Senate from Hawaii after having served seven consecutive terms in the U.S. House of Representatives. *(Also see entry dated October 8, 1916.)*

Native Hawaiian Daniel K. Akaka was elected by 80 percent of the vote to the U.S. House of Representatives from Hawaii; it was the first of seven terms he would serve.

Chinese American author Maxine Hong Kingston published *The Woman Warrior,* in which she portrayed the conflicting cultural messages sent to her as she forged her identity as a Chinese American woman.

Filipino American author and illustrator José Aruego was named the Outstanding Filipino Abroad in the Arts by the Philippine government. *(Also see entry dated 1970.)*

Alfred Wong was the first Asian/Pacific American appointed marshal of the U.S. Supreme Court. He was also the first to serve as special agent in the White House Secret Service.

The Organization of PanAsian American Women (PANASIA) was founded to provide a voice for the concerns of Asian Pacific American women. PANASIA seeks to develop leadership skills and to maintain a national communications network. The group is headquartered in Washington, D.C.

Eduardo Manlapit became the first Filipino American county executive in the United States, serving as mayor of Kauai, an island in the northwest Hawaii.

Samuel Ting (1936–) shared the Nobel Prize in physics with Burton Richter for the discovery of a new particle called j/psi.

Executive Order 9066, responsible for the detention of persons of Japanese ancestry during World War II, was officially rescinded. *(Also see entry dated February 19, 1942.)*

S. I. Hayakawa was elected to the U.S. Senate, becoming the first immigrant (he was born in Canada) of Japanese ancestry elected to Congress.

Years of Infamy: The Untold Story of America's Concentration Camps, by Michiko Nishiura Weglyn, was published. The book exposed the horror of

Senator S. I. Hayakawa

the imprisonment of Americans of Japanese descent in internment camps during World War II and the abuses of power in the U.S. government that failed to protect the rights of these American citizens. *(Also see entry dated February 19, 1942.)*

1977   Morikami Park, the Museum of Japanese Culture, and Japanese Gardens, were opened to the public on land given to Palm Beach County, Florida, by Japanese American George Morikami. *(Also see entry dated 1973.)*

Morikami had hired on as an indentured worker in the Yamato (farming) Colony in Boca Raton, Florida, in 1906. He eventually became a millionaire

114

Patsy Mink talks with Kenneth Young of the labor organization, AFL-CIO

landowner and fulfilled his dream of becoming a naturalized citizen in 1967. *(Also see entry dated 1904.)*

Patsy Takemoto Mink was appointed assistant secretary of state in Oceans and International Environment and Scientific Affairs by President Jimmy Carter. *(Also see entry dated 1964.)*

Russell C. Leong cofounded the *Amerasia Journal* with Asian American social scientist Don Nakanishi and became its first editor. The journal has become a strong voice in Asian American literature and scholarship.

The Natori Company was founded by Filipina American Josie Cruz Natori and her husband Kenneth Natori to import Philippine products. The company today is a $40 million fashion empire, launched when the Natoris imported a hand-embroidered blouse and soon found themselves in the lingerie business.

January 19. Iva Toguri D'Aquino, also known as Tokyo Rose, was pardoned by President Gerald Ford. *(Also see entry dated October 7, 1949.)*

October. President Jimmy Carter appointed Thomas Tang, a Chinese American, to the U.S. Court of Appeals for the Ninth Circuit, making Tang the highest-ranking Chinese American federal judge. The Ninth Circuit serves nine western states.

Judge Thomas Tang

1978 Robert Matsui was elected to the U.S. Congress as the the representative from California's fifth district, which comprises the Sacramento area. *(Also see entry dated 1971.)*

Thousands of "boat people" arrived from Vietnam, a second wave of refugees risking their lives in small, leaky vessels hoping to find a better life in the United States. *(Also see entry dated April 30, 1975.)*

Asian Indian American Zubin Mehta became the music director of the New York Philharmonic, a post he would hold for thirteen years. *(Also see entry dated 1962.)*

Toshiko Akiyoshi, Japanese American jazz pianist and band leader of the band Best Big Jazz Band, was named Best Arranger in the *Down Beat* magazine Readers' Poll.

The East Wing of the National Gallery of Art in Washington, D.C., designed by Chinese American architect I. M. Pei, was dedicated. *(Also see entry dated April 26, 1917.)*

The Walker Art Center in Minneapolis, Minnesota, staged a retrospective of the work of Japanese American sculptor Isamu Noguchi. *(Also see entry dated 1904.)*

House Joint Resolution 10007 officially recognized Asian/Pacific American Heritage Week.

The Japanese American Citizens League national convention, held in Salt Lake City, Utah, resolved to seek $25,000 for each detainee (Japanese Americans held in U.S. detention camps during World War II) and launched a national redress (reparations) campaign. *(Also see entry dated February 19, 1942.)*

November 25. The first Day of Remembrance pilgrimage and program were held at the former temporary detention camp site at Puyallup, Washington. *(Also see entry dated February 19, 1942.)*

1979   In Los Angeles, California, Chinese American John Ta-Chuan Fang established *Asian Week*, a national weekly English-language newspaper covering Asian American news.

The Indochina Resource Action Center (IRAC) was founded in Washington, D.C., to help refugee organizations establish programs in communities around the United States. IRAC changed its name to Southeast Asian Resource Action Center (SEARAC) to reflect the change in terminology used in referring to refugees from Vietnam, Cambodia, and Laos. SEARAC publishes reports on issues affecting refugees and sponsors training workshops for community organizations serving refugees.

Ruthann Lum McCunn, of Chinese and Scottish descent, published *An Illustrated History of the Chinese in America,* which has been used as a college textbook.

The John F. Kennedy Library, designed by Chinese American architect I. M. Pei, was dedicated in Cambridge, Massachusetts. The project had taken fifteen years to complete and had gone through three different designs for three different sites. *(Also see entry dated April 26, 1917.)*

A national Asian/Pacific American movement to unify all Asian Americans began under the leadership of Mary and Mark Au. Their Asian American Heritage Council, Inc., was intended to educate communities about cultural and civil rights issues. The first festival of Asian American unity was held on the Washington Monument grounds in Washington, D.C.

The National Council for Japanese American Redress was formed in Seattle, Washington. Its goal was to effect a judicial remedy for wartime detention. *(Also see entry dated February 19, 1942.)*

February 19. On the anniversary of the signing of Executive Order 9066, the cities of San Francisco and San Bruno, California, proclaimed a day of remembrance and marked the occasion with a pilgrimage to the Tanforan camp in San Bruno. Other cities, counties, and states also proclaimed this a day of remembrance.

1980   The Refugee Act of 1980 was signed into law by President Jimmy Carter; it enabled greater numbers of refugees to enter the United States. An Office of Refugee Resettlement was established within the Department of Health and Human Services to assist in administering the program.

Asian/Pacific Americans, according to the U.S. Census Bureau, numbered 3.5 million, or 1.5 percent of the total U.S. population, double the 1970 figure. It was the first time Asian Indians were counted in the census as Asians, which gave them official minority status.

The New York Chinatown History Project was launched in New York City to reclaim, preserve, and share the history and culture of Chinese Americans in the metropolitan New York area. The project evolved into the Chinatown History Museum, featuring interactive exhibits, lectures, symposia, readings, and family events. The museum, located at 70 Mulberry Street in the heart of New York's Chinatown, houses a library and bookstore in addition to its exhibit halls.

Asian American Population in 1980

Population category	Number
Total U.S. population	226,545,805
Total Asian American population	3,455,421
Chinese	812,178
Filipino (from the Philippines)	781,894
Asian Indian	387,223
Japanese	716,331
Korean	357,393
Vietnamese	245,025

Source: U.S. Bureau of Census, Decennial Censuses of Population

The National Coalition for Redress/Reparations was formed in Los Angeles and San Francisco. It provided an activist workforce for the redress campaign for Japanese Americans held in internment camps during World War II. Bay Area Attorneys for Redress also began meeting in the San Francisco area. Three years later, the group was restructured as the Committee to Reverse the Japanese American Wartime Cases to handle the petitions of Gordon Hirabayashi, Fred Korematsu, and Minoru Yasui. Attorneys in the Pacific Northwest joined the group. *(Also see entries dated February 19, 1942, March 28, 1942, May 5, 1942, and May 30, 1942.)*

Pakistani American Safi Qureshey, along with Thomas Yuen and Albert Wong, pooled $2,000 in resources to found AST Research. By 1992, Qureshey was the only remaining partner, and AST Research had appeared on the *Fortune* 500 list of leading U.S. companies as the fourth-largest producer of personal computers after IBM, Apple, and Compaq.

July 31. The Commission on Wartime Relocation and Internment of Civilians began gathering facts to determine if any wrong had been committed against U.S. citizens, most of them Japanese, affected by Executive Order 9066. *(Also see entry dated February 19, 1942.)*

1981   Chinese American architect and sculptor Maya Lin submitted the winning design for the Vietnam Veterans Memorial in Washington, D.C. The design featured two highly polished walls of black granite, set in a "V" shape and

Maya Lin, designer of the Vietnam Veterans Memorial

inscribed with the names of the almost 58,000 dead or missing veterans of the Vietnam War. Lin's design was chosen from 1,420 entries. At the time, she was an undergraduate at Yale University in New Haven, Connecticut. She was later awarded an honorary doctorate for her efforts.

Ming Erh Chang was the first Asian/Pacific American promoted to rank of rear admiral, after having held major command positions in the U.S. Navy.

Bette Bao Lord published *Spring Moon,* which would soon become a best-seller and National Book Award nominee. The book offered a fictional account of Bao Lord's return, as an adult, to China, the place of her birth. *(Also see entry dated 1964.)*

The U.S. Immigration and Naturalization Service granted Taiwan a separate immigration quota from that of mainland China in order to facilitate family reunifications.

The Ku Klux Klan (a post-Civil War secret society advocating white supremacy—a belief that whites are superior to people of other races) of Texas burned boats, symbolizing their opposition to Vietnamese immigration and resettlement programs.

The Asian American Journalists Association was founded by Tritia Toyota, television journalist, and Bill Sing, a reporter with the *Los Angeles Times.*

July 14. The first of ten public hearings held across the United States by the Commission on Wartime Relocation and Internment of Civilians commenced in Washington, D.C. The committee heard from over 750 witnesses on the question of the legitimacy of detaining Japanese Americans in internment camps during World War II. *(Also see entry dated February 19, 1942.)*

August 5. Senator S. I. Hayakawa of California, the son of Japanese immigrants, opposed reparations for Japanese Americans who had been interned in relocation camps during World War II. *(Also see entries dated February 19, 1942, and 1976.)*

Even though he conceded that the civil rights of the internees had been violated, Hayakawa felt that the internment was justifiable due to the mood of panic at the time. *(Also see entry dated 1976.)*

Subrahmanyan Chandrasekhar

1982 After spending nine years in prison for a killing he did not commit, Korean immigrant Chol Soo Lee was acquitted by a San Francisco jury.

The dishonorable discharges of the Fort McClellan protesters and members of the 1800th General Services Battalion were changed to honorable and their prison records erased. Over 100 *nisei* (children of Japanese immigrants) soldiers had refused combat training to protest their families' incarceration in internment camps during World War II. *(Also see entries dated February 19, 1942, and March 24, 1944.)*

The California legislature agreed to pay $5,000 restitution to 314 Japanese American state employees who had been forced to leave their jobs in 1942. In subsequent years, similar restitutions were granted by other cities, counties, and states on the West Coast. *(Also see entry dated April 2, 1942.)*

Isamu Noguchi, Japanese American sculptor and architect, received the Edward MacDowell Medal for outstanding lifetime contribution to the arts. *(Also see entry dated 1904.)*

June 22. Vincent Chin, a twenty-seven-year-old Chinese American in Detroit, Michigan, was bludgeoned to death with a baseball bat by two unemployed autoworkers who blamed layoffs in the auto industry on the Japanese auto industry. The two assailants had mistaken Chin for a Japanese.

Architect I. M. Pei

1983 Subrahmanyan Chandrasekhar (1910–1995) was awarded the Nobel Prize in physics, with William A. Fowler. Chandrasekhar's prizewinning theory concerned the structure of white dwarf stars. It was pioneering work that laid the groundwork for the eventual discovery of black holes.

Chandrasekhar was born in Lahore, India (in present day Pakistan), in 1910. After studying in India, he attended Cambridge University in England where he earned a Ph.D. in physics. He moved to the United States in 1936 to work at the University of Chicago and the Yerkes Observatory in Williams Bay, Wisconsin. Chandrasekhar became a U.S. citizen in 1953; he died in August 1995.

Chinese American architect I. M. Pei was named Laureate of the Prizker Architecture Prize. With this $100,000 award, he established a scholarship fund for Chinese students to study architecture in the United States, provided that they would return to China to practice what they had learned. *(Also see entry dated April 26, 1917.)*

In Fort Dodge, Iowa, a Laotian immigrant named Thong Soukaseume was assaulted by a man yelling "Remember Pearl Harbor" and "Go back to Japan, you Kamikaze pilot." (Kamikaze [the word means "divine wind" in Japanese] were members of a Japanese air attack corps in World War II assigned to make suicidal crashes on targets, usually enemy ships.)

A congressional committee issued a report criticizing the government's incarceration of 120,000 Japanese Americans during World War II. *(Also see entry dated February 19, 1942.)*

In an expression of humanitarian concern for abandoned Amerasian children (children with one American parent, usually the father, and one Asian parent, usually the mother) of U.S. servicemen, Congress authorized the admission into the United States of Amerasian children from Korea, Vietnam, and Thailand.

Asian American communities across the country were outraged by the probation sentence given to the two men who beat Chinese American Vincent Chin to death in Detroit. A federal grand jury later indicted the two men on federal civil rights charges. A trial on federal charges would be held in June 1984. *(Also see entry dated June 22, 1982.)*

June 23. The report by the Commission of Wartime Relocation and Internment of Civilians, *Personal Justice Denied,* was released. The commission concluded that the exclusion of Japanese Americans from American society, the expulsion of Japanese Americans from their homes, and the incarceration of Japanese Americans in internment camps were not justified by military necessity, and that the decision had been based on racial prejudice, war hysteria, and a failure of political leadership. The authors of the report recommended that Congress pass a joint resolution, to be signed by the president, recognizing the grave injustice done to Japanese Americans and offering an official apology from the U.S. government. They also recommended a one-time compensatory payment of $20,000 to each of the approximately 60,000 surviving persons exiled from their places of residence and imprisoned by Executive Order 9066. *(Also see entries dated February 19, 1942, and July 14, 1981.)*

October 4. In response to a petition for a writ of error by Fred Korematsu, who defied the order to relocate to an internment camp in 1942, the Federal District

Court of San Francisco reversed Korematsu's original conviction and ruled that the government had no justification for issuing the internment orders. *(Also see entry dated May 30, 1942.)*

October 6. Redress bill HR 4110 was introduced in the House of Representatives by Majority Leader Jim Wright of Texas and seventy-two cosponsors in order to implement the recommendations of the Commission of Wartime Relocation and Internment of Civilians. *(Also see entry dated June 23, 1983.)*

November 6. Senator "Spark" Masayuki Matsunaga introduced redress Senate bill 2216 with thirteen cosponsors. *(Also see entry dated October 8, 1916.)*

1984

In Davis, California, Thong Hy Huynh was stabbed to death on the Davis High School grounds during a fight with two white students who had been taunting Huynh and three other Vietnamese students with racial epithets for weeks.

Chinese American skater Tiffany Chin placed fourth in figure skating at the Winter Olympics in Sarajevo, Yugoslavia.

Greg Louganis, a Samoan American diver, won the Gold Medal in platform diving at the Summer Olympics in Los Angeles. He became the first diver in history to break the 700-point mark, with a score of 710.91. Louganis also won the Gold Medal in springboard diving, becoming the first man in fifty-six years to win both diving titles at the same Olympics. *(Also see entries dated 1971 and 1988.)*

Tommy Kono, a Japanese American weightlifting Gold Medalist, was voted the greatest weightlifter of all time by the International Weightlifting Federation. Kono was born in Sacramento, California, and moved to Hawaii in 1952. *(Also see entry dated 1952.)*

Chinese American Bette Bao Lord published her first children's book, *In the Year of the Boar and Jackie Robinson,* a fictionalized account of her first year in America. *(Also see entry dated 1964.)*

Ronald Ebens was found guilty of violating Vincent Chin's civil rights, and was sentenced to twenty-five years in prison. He appealed the case. *(Also see entries dated June 22, 1982, 1983, and 1987.)*

S. B. Woo was elected lieutenant governor of Delaware, the highest state office attained by an Asian American.

Cathy-Lynn Song won the Yale Series of Younger Poets Award for her volume of poetry *Picture Bride*.

The California state legislature proclaimed that "February 19, 1984, and February 19th of each year thereafter be recognized as 'A Day of Remembrance,' a time set aside so that Californians might reflect upon their shared responsibility to uphold the Constitution and moral rights of all individuals at all times." *(Also see entry dated February 19, 1942.)*

S. B. WOO

1985   *Asian Week* reported that there were 4.8 million Asians in the United States and that this population would reach 6.5 million by 1990.

A Vietnamese Chinese restaurant owner in Boston, Massachusetts, was beaten by two white youths. The words "Gook sucks" were scratched into the restaurant window. ("Gook" is a vulgar, derogatory slang term for Asians.)

Diver Greg Louganis won the Sullivan Award, presented by the Amateur Athletic Union (AAU) to the outstanding amateur athlete of the year. *(Also see entry dated 1984.)*

Filipina American Irene Natividad was the first Asian American to be elected to head the National Women's Political Caucus. The Caucus was founded in 1971 by a small group of feminists that included former congresswomen Bella

Chinese American poet Him Mark Lai reads poetry carved by Chinese immigrants into the walls of the U.S. Immigration Station at Angel Island during their detention

Abzug, Shirley Chisholm, and Patsy Mink in order to focus on putting women into elected and appointed political offices. *(Also see entry dated 1964.)*

Beulah Quo, Chinese American actor, joined the cast of the daytime soap opera *General Hospital* as Olin, a hip housekeeper. Quo was the only Asian American actor whose story line recurred on a soap opera over several years, lasting until 1991.

Kent Nagano, Japanese American conductor, won a Seaver/National Endowment for the Arts Conductor's Award, a grant made to extraordinarily promising American conductors.

An exhibit recounting the experiences of early Chinese immigrants to the United States was mounted at Angel Island Immigration Station, San Francisco, California. Angel Island had served as the principal entry point for

Dr. Haing S. Ngor in the film *The Killing Fields*, and with his Oscar

immigrants arriving on the West Coast. Nearly all these immigrants were from Asia or the Pacific Islands.

January 24. Lt. Col. Ellison Onizuka flew as a missions specialist on STS 51-c, the first space shuttle mission, thus becoming the first Asian American in space. *(Also see entries dated June 24, 1946, and January 28, 1986.)*

March 25. Dr. Haing S. Ngor won an Oscar as best supporting actor at the fifty-seventh Annual Academy Awards for his first acting role in *The Killing Fields*. Ngor, the son of a Khmer (Cambodian ethnic group) mother and an ethnic Chinese father, became the first Asian American ever to receive an Oscar for acting.

April 29–May 5. Dr. Taylor Wang, a Chinese American physicist, became the second Asian American to travel in space when he flew aboard the shuttle *Challenger*.

October. A federal district court in Portland, Oregon, overturned Minoru Yasui's conviction for violating a curfew order during World War II. *(Also see entry dated March 28, 1942.)*

1986   Chinese American Dr. Yuan T. Lee, professor at the University of California, Berkeley, was awarded the Nobel Prize in chemistry, along with Dudley R. Herschbach, for his research into the nature of chemical reactions.

Asian Indian American Ismail Merchant, with James Ivory, produced a film adaptation of E. M. Forster's *A Room with a View* that brought him great acclaim.

A federal district court in Seattle invalidated Gordon Hirabayashi's 1942 conviction for violating wartime internment orders. *(Also see entry dated June 21, 1943.)*

The garment industry in New York City employed 22,000 Chinese workers in 550 unionized factories. Chinese immigrant women clustered in the garment industry, working as seamstresses, partly due to their lack of English–speaking skills, but also because they could bring their infants to work with them.

January 28. Lt. Col. Ellison Onizuka, the first Asian American astronaut, perished along with six other crew members when the space shuttle *Challenger* exploded shortly after takeoff. *(Also see entry dated January 24, 1985.)*

July 4. Chinese American architect I. M. Pei was one of twelve foreign-born Americans to receive the Medal of Liberty from President Ronald Reagan at the centennial celebration commemorating the Statue of Liberty. *(Also see entry dated April 26, 1917.)*

July. Fourteen-year-old Japanese American violinist Midori was performing Leonard Bernstein's "Serenade" at the Tanglewood Music Festival in Massachusetts when her E-string broke. She picked up the concertmaster's violin and continued, but the E-string broke again. She continued with the assistant concertmaster's instrument and finished her performance flawlessly to a massive ovation.

1987   Bill HR442, which would become the Civil Liberties Act of 1988, was submitted to the House of Representatives on January 6, 1987. Bill S1009, "a bill to accept the findings and implement recommendations of the Commission of Wartime Relocation and Internment of Civilians," was submitted to the Senate on April 10, 1987. *(Also see entry June 23, 1983.)*

Patricia Saiki was the first Republican to represent Hawaii in the U.S. House of Representatives. She served until 1991.

Ajai Singh "Sonny" Mehta became head of Alfred A. Knopf, a division of Random House publishing. As of 1995, Knopf writers had won more Nobel Prizes in literature than those of any other publisher.

Hoang Nhu Tran, a Vietnamese refugee, graduated first in his class from the United States Air Force Academy and became a Rhodes scholar (recipient of a prestigious scholarship founded under the will of British colonial administrator Cecil Rhodes).

A group of youths attacked and killed Navroze Mody, an Indian man, in Jersey City, New Jersey. The youths were allegedly affiliated with the "Dotbusters," a gang whose name is a reference to the distinctive "dot" worn on the foreheads of many Indian women.

A Filipino American family was taunted and harassed after moving into a mostly white neighborhood in Queens, New York. White youths hurled objects at family members and shouted gibberish, attempting to imitate the Filipino language, Tagalog, the family's native tongue.

Ronald Ebens appealed his twenty-five-year prison sentence for the 1982 murder of Vincent Chin in the U.S. Appellate Court in Cincinnati, Ohio. Ebens was acquitted of the murder and never spent a single day in jail. *(Also see entries dated June 22, 1982, and 1984.)*

President Ronald Reagan appointed Asian Indian American Joy Cherian to the U.S. Equal Employment Opportunity Commission.

A woman works at her sewing machine at a New York garment shop while her child sits in a swing

May 4. Senator Daniel Inouye, chairman of the Senate Select Committee investigating the Iran-Contra affair, convened joint House and Senate investigative hearings. The Iran-contra scandal was a secret arrangement carried out by top officials in Ronald Reagan's administration. These officials obtained funds by selling arms to Iran and then used these funds to aid the contras who were conducting guerrilla warfare against the socialist Sandinista government in Nicaragua. Congress had passed legislation that prohibited any government agency from providing military aid to the contras. Inouye had also served as a member of the Senate Select Committee investing Watergate. During the Iran-Contra probe, Inouye became the target of racial slurs, including telegrams and phone calls telling the American-born senator to "go back home to Japan where you belong." *(Also see entry dated September 7, 1924.)*

June 1. The Supreme Court, in an 8-0 vote, sent the lawsuit stemming from the detention of Japanese Americans during World War II back to a lower court. No ruling was made. The Court stated that the case had been improperly heard by the District of Columbia Court of Appeals and should instead have come before the Federal Circuit Court of Appeals. *(Also see February 19, 1942.)*

October 1. The Japanese American exhibit opened at the Smithsonian Institution's National Museum of American History, in Washington, D.C.

October–November. The Immigration Reform and Control Act of 1986 was passed by the House of Representatives on October 15, 1987, passed by the Senate on October 17, 1987, and signed by President Ronald Reagan on November 6, 1987. This act allowed aliens who could prove that they were in the United States prior to January 1, 1982, to apply for temporary status and become U.S. citizens seven years after the time of application. There were no changes in the preference system that allowed for family reunification. *(Also see entry dated 1981.)*

1988   Greg Louganis won Gold Medals in both platform and springboard diving at the Summer Olympic Games in Seoul, South Korea. Louganis thus became the first athlete to win two diving medals in successive Olympics. He also won the Olympic Spirit Award, designating him the most inspiring athlete among the 9,600 competing in Seoul.

During the competition, Louganis hit his head on the diving board, suffering a three-inch gash. But he courageously went on to complete the competition. In 1995, however, Louganis revealed that he had kept secret a controversial medical condition during the 1988 Olympics. Prior to the competition, he had tested positive for

HIV, the virus that causes Acquired Immune Deficiency Syndrome (AIDS). No one except Louganis and his coach were aware of the test results. Despite some criticism for not revealing his medical condition, Louganis's repu-tation as the most inspiring athlete at the 1988 Olympics rests on his remarkable accomplishments there. *(Also see entries dated 1971 and 1984.)*

David Henry Hwang's Broadway play *M. Butterfly* won the prestigious Tony Award. The production, which grossed $35 million, also won the Drama Desk, Outer Critics Circle, and John Gassner awards. The drama (based on a true story) is about a male French diplomat who falls in love with an female opera singer who is really a man posing as a woman. Playwright Hwang is Chinese American. His father was the first Asian American to found a national bank.

Greg Louganis

Ladies Home Journal named California secretary of state March Fong Eu one of America's "100 Most Important Women." *(Also see entry dated 1966.)*

In Berkeley, California, racist graffiti proclaiming "Japs and Chinks Only!" was found on a door of the Ethnic Studies Department of the University of California. ("Jap" and "Chink" are vulgar, derogatory slang terms for Japanese and Chinese.)

Congressman Norman Mineta signing the Redress Bill. Standing at right is Congressman Robert Matsui

Jahja Ling was one of three conductors to receive the Seaver/National Endowment for the Arts Conductor's Award.

Ling was born in Jakarta, Indonesia, to parents of Chinese descent. Musically talented even as a child, he attended the Jakarta Music School. Upon his graduation, he received a Rockefeller grant to study at the famed Juilliard School of Music in New York City. He eventually came to hold two posts: resident conductor of the Cleveland Orchestra and music director of the Florida Orchestra.

July 27. The U.S. Senate passed revised redress bill HR 4110. *(Also see entry dated November 6, 1983.)*

August 4. The U.S. House of Representatives passed revised redress bill HR 4110 despite the strong opposition of President Ronald Reagan. *(Also see entries dated June 23, 1983, and October 6, 1983.)*

August 10. The Civil Liberties Act of 1988 (redress bill HR 4110, which would provide reparation to Japanese Americans interned during World War II) was signed by President Ronald Reagan. The bill gave each surviving internee a tax-free payment of $20,000 and a letter of apology from the U.S. government. *(Also see entry dated February 19, 1942.)*

1989 The Coalition of Asian Pacific Americans, the first Asian Pacific political action committee, was founded.

Sichan Siv

Cambodian refugee Sichan Siv was appointed deputy assistant to President George Bush, a post he held until 1992. After fleeing the Khmer Rouge (Communists) in Phnom Penh, the capital of Cambodia, during the Vietnam War, Siv finally arrived in the United States in 1976. He rose to become the highest-ranking Asian American on the White House staff just thirteen years later.

Elaine L. Chao was appointed as deputy secretary of the Department of Transportation in President George Bush's cabinet. *(Also see entry dated 1993.)*

The Boy of the Three-Year Nap by Dianne Snyder with illustrations by Japanese American artist Allen Say (1937–), won the coveted Caldecott Honor award for picture books.

Patrick Purdy fired 105 rounds from an assault rifle at children in an elementary schoolyard in Stockton, California, killing five Southeast Asian children and then himself. Purdy had blamed all minorities for his failings, and targeted Southeast Asians for his homicidal plans.

Two white men killed twenty-four-year-old Ming Hai "Jim" Loo, a Chinese American man, outside a pool hall in Raleigh, North Carolina, after shouting "We shouldn't put up with Vietnamese in our country."

Julia Chang Bloch was named ambassador to Nepal by President George Bush, making her the first Asian American ambassador in U.S. history.

Manny Crisostomo, a native of Guam, won a Pulitzer Prize in feature photography for his work in the *Detroit Free Press*.

Chinese American Michael Chang won the French Open tennis tournament, the youngest male and the first American winner since 1955. He won the title by defeating Ivan Lendl, the world's top-ranked player.

Sarah Chang, an eight-year-old violinist, played as a surprise

Cover for *The Boy of the Three-Year Nap*, illustrated by Allen Say

Tennis superstar Michael Chang

Violinist Sarah Chang

guest soloist with the New York Philharmonic at the invitation of conductor Zubin Mehta. *(Also see entry dated 1962.)*

Chang, the daughter of Korean immigrants who came to the United States in 1979, began performing at the age of five, and at age six began taking lessons at the prestigious Juilliard School of Music in New York City. She would go on to perform with some of the world's most renowned orchestras and conductors.

The documentary film, *Who Killed Vincent Chin?* was nominated for an Academy Award for best feature documentary. Christine Choy, co-producer and director with Renee Tajima, has produced, directed, and acted as cinematographer on approximately fifty films in her two-decade career as a pioneer Asian American filmmaker. *(Also see entry dated June 22, 1982.)*

Christine Choy directing a scene for her documentary *Who Killed Vincent Chin?*

Strangers from a Different Shore: A History of Asian Americans, by Ronald Takaki, received a number of awards, including a Pulitzer Prize nomination for nonfiction, the Gold Medal for nonfiction from the Commonwealth Club of California, and Notable Book of 1989 honors from the *New York Times Book Review.*

The Joy Luck Club, by Amy Tan, a second-generation Chinese American, was published and became a blockbuster on the *New York Times* best-seller list from April through November. The book, Tan's first, was a finalist for the National Book Award and the National Book Critics Circle Award. It would later be made into a critically acclaimed film with an all-Asian cast.

September 21. A bill to make redress funding (to compensate Japanese Americans interned during World War II) an entitlement program (a government program that gives benefits to members of specific groups) was signed by President George Bush. *(Also see entries dated February 19, 1982, and August 10, 1988.)*

Amy Tan

1990 Democrat Daniel K. Akaka, member of the U.S. House of Representatives, was appointed to fill the Senate seat of Senator "Spark" Masayaki Matsunaga after Matsunaga's death. Akaka was the first Native Hawaiian to serve in the U.S. Senate. In fact, Akaka was so dedicated to his work on behalf of Hawaii that he delayed his acceptance of the appointment so that he could make sure that several projects important to the state would be advanced by the House Appropriations Committee. *(Also see entries dated October 8, 1916, and 1976.)*

Patsy Takemoto Mink was elected to serve the remainder of Daniel Akaka's unexpired term in the U.S. House of Representatives. *(Also see entry dated 1964.)*

Republican Cheryl Lau, a Native Hawaiian, was elected secretary of state of Nevada.

Asian American Population in 1990

Population category	Number
Total U.S. population	248,709,873
Total Asian American population	7,273,662
Chinese	1,645,472
Filipino (from the Philippines)	1,406,770
Asian Indian	815,447
Japanese	847,562
Korean	798,849
Vietnamese	614,547

Source: U.S. Bureau of Census, Decennial Censuses of Population

David Valderrama became the first Filipino American elected official in the United States when he was elected delegate of the Maryland General Assembly. He was also the first probate judge in the United States of Filipino ancestry.

Two white men assaulted Xan Than Ly, a Laotian American restaurant employee in Yuba City, California, after seeing him driving with two white female co-workers who had asked for a ride. Using a hammer, they attacked Ly and the women, breaking the windows of Ly's truck.

Chinese American architect I. M. Pei received the commission to design the Rock and Roll Hall of Fame and Museum in Cleveland, Ohio. (*Also see entry dated April 26, 1917.*)

The myth of the "Model Minority" gained prominence during the 1990s. This idea, that all Asian Pacific Americans are part of a homogeneous group of highly intelligent, exceedingly successful people who have achieved the American dream, was held by many mainstream Americans. The idea became a troubling stereotype for many reasons. One is that low priority has been given to support for social service programs for Asian Pacific Americans; another is that, by depicting Asian Americans as successful where other minority groups are not, tensions and resentment between Asian Americans and other groups is created; yet another is that unreasonable expectations are placed on all people of Asian descent to be successful.

George Bush signs a proclamation declaring May as Asian/Pacific American Heritage Month

President George Bush extended the celebration of Asian/Pacific American heritage to a month in his proclamation designating May 1990 as Asian/Pacific American Heritage Month. Several prominent Asian Americans joined him for the ceremonial signing of the proclamation in the Rose Garden at the White House. Pictured with President Bush, from left to right, are Taylor Wang, Chinese American astronaut; Virginia Cha, 1989 Miss Maryland and first runner-up in the Miss America pageant; I. M. Pei, Chinese American architect; Sammy Lee, Korean American Olympic diver and physician; Nancy Kwan, Chinese American actress; and Tsung-Dao Lee, Chinese American Nobel Prize winner in physics.

Hawaii commemorated the 100th anniversary of the birth of Native Hawaiian Olympic swimmer and world-class surfer Duke Kahanamoku by dedicating a

141

ASIAN/PACIFIC AMERICAN
HERITAGE MONTH, 1991 AND 1992

By the President of the United States of America

A Proclamation

With characteristic clarity and force, Walt Whitman wrote: "The United States themselves are essentially the greatest poem . . . . Here is not merely a nation but a teeming nation of nations." Those immortal words eloquently describe America's ethnic diversity — a diversity we celebrate with pride during Asian/Pacific American Heritage Month.

The Asian/Pacific American heritage is marked by its richness and depth. The world marvels at the wealth of ancient art and philosophy, the fine craftsmanship, and the colorful literature and folklore that have sprung from Asia and the Pacific islands. Whether they trace their roots to places like Cambodia, Vietnam, Korea, the Philippines, and the Marshall Islands or cherish their identities as natives of Hawaii and Guam, all Asian and Pacific Americans can take pride in this celebration of their heritage.

By preserving the time-honored customs and traditions of their ancestral homelands, Americans of Asian and Pacific descent have greatly enriched our Nation's culture. They have also made many outstanding contributions to American history. Indeed, this country's westward expansion and economic development were greatly influenced by thousands of Chinese and other Asians who immigrated during the 19th century. Today recent immigrants from South Asia are giving our Nation new appreciation for that region of the world.

Over the years — and often in the face of great obstacles — Asian and Pacific Americans have worked hard to reap the rewards of freedom and opportunity. Many have arrived in the United States after long and arduous journeys, escaping tyranny and oppression with little more than the clothes on their backs. Yet, believing in America's promise of liberty and justice for all and imbued with a strong sense of self-discipline, sacrifice, courage, and honor, they have steadily advanced, earning the respect and admiration of their fellow citizens. Today we give special and long-overdue recognition to the nisei who fought for our country in Europe during World War II. During one of America's darker hours, they affirmed the patriotism and loyalty of Japanese Americans and, in so doing, taught us an important lesson about tolerance and justice.

Time and again throughout our Nation's history, Asian and Pacific Americans have proved their devotion to the ideals of freedom and democratic government. Those ideals animate and guide our policies toward Asia and the Pacific today. The economic dynamism of the Pacific Rim is a crucial source of growth for the global economy, and the United States will continue working to promote economic cooperation and the expansion of free markets throughout the region. The United States also remains committed to the security of our allies and to the advancement of human rights throughout Asia and the Pacific.

The political and economic ties that exist between the United States and countries in Asia and the Pacific are fortified by strong bonds of kinship and culture. All Americans are enriched by those ties, and thus we proudly unite in observing Asian/Pacific American Heritage Month.

The Congress, by House Joint Resolution 173, has designated May 1991 and May 1992 as "Asian/Pacific American Heritage Month" and has authorized and requested the President to issue a proclamation in observance of these occasions.

NOW, THEREFORE, I, GEORGE BUSH, President of the United States of America, do hereby proclaim the months of May 1991 and May 1992 as Asian/Pacific American Heritage Month. I call upon the people of the United States to observe these occasions with appropriate programs, ceremonies, and activities.

IN WITNESS WHEREOF, I have hereunto set my hand this sixth day of May, in the year of our Lord nineteen hundred and ninety-one, and of the Independence of the United States of America the two hundred and fifteenth.

Ay Bush

Asian/Pacific American Heritage Month Proclamation

nine-foot bronze statue with a twelve-foot surfboard at its side on Waikiki Beach, "The Bronze Duke of Waikiki." *(Also see entry dated August 26, 1890.)*

Vera Wang opened her Vera Wang Bridal House in New York City. She had designed her own wedding gown in 1989 after a futile search for one she liked. Wang also started a separate couture business, designing gowns for actresses such as Sharon Stone and Holly Hunter (couture is the business of designing fashionable, custom-made women's clothing). In 1994 she would be elected to the elite Council of Fashion Designers of America.

Cover of Allen Say's *El Chino*

Japanese American golfer David Ishii won the Hawaiian Open PGA (Professional Golfers Association) tournament.

Allen Say, Japanese American author and illustrator, published the critically acclaimed *El Chino*, the story of the first Chinese bullfighter. *(Also see entry dated 1989.)*

Doctor and AIDS researcher David D. Ho was named head of the Aaron Diamond AIDS Research Center in New York City, one of the largest facilities of its kind in the world. Ho, recognized as one of the leading authorities on AIDS, began research on the disease in 1984.

April 23. The U.S. Congress passed the Hate Crimes Statistics Act to allow the gathering and publication of data concerning crimes against persons based on their racial characteristics.

143

Attorney General Richard Thornburgh presenting $20,000 checks to three elderly Japanese Americans interned during World War II

October 9. The first redress (reparations) checks and government apologies were presented by U.S. Attorney General Richard Thornburgh to recipients at a ceremony at the Justice Department in Washington, D.C. *(Also see entry dated August 10, 1988.)*

1991   Major General John Liu Fugh achieved the position of judge advocate general (senior legal officer) of the army, a post he would hold until his retirement in 1993. Major Fugh was the first Chinese American to attain general officer status in the military.

An act intended to amend the Civil Rights Act of 1964 was passed by Congress to define procedures for taking legal action against discrimination in the workplace. *(Also see entry dated 1964.)*

Steven Okazaki with his Academy Award for *Days of Waiting*

The Academy Award for best documentary short subject was awarded to Steven Okazaki for *Days of Waiting,* the story of artist Estelle Ishigo, a Caucasian woman who chose internment over separation from her Japanese American husband. *(Also see entry dated February 19, 1942.)*

Japanese American photojournalist Paul Kuroda was named Newspaper Photographer of the Year by the National Press Photographers Association and the University of Missouri School of Journalism.

Chinese American Gus Lee (born in 1946) published the semi-autobiographical novel *China Boy,* in which he introduced the character of Kai Tin, the American-born son of Chinese parents. It was a Literary Guild selection and one of the *New York Times'* "Best 100 for 1991."

Lee, an attorney, had never attempted to write fiction before. He wrote *China Boy* at his daughter's request that he write a family journal. He would publish the second installment of Kai Ting's story, *Honor and Duty*, in 1994.

Asian Indian American Dinesh D'Souza published *Illiberal Education: The Politics of Race and Sex on Campus*. D'Souza's conservative views fueled the ongoing debates about political correctness (a belief that language and practices which could offend certain groups of people should be eliminated) and the role of the university in society. The book became a bestseller and made D'Souza a much-in-demand lecturer and opinion writer.

House Joint Resolution 173, introduced by Congressman Frank Horton, was passed by the House of Representatives on April 24, 1991, by the Senate on April 25, 1991, and approved by President George Bush on May 6, 1991. It designated May 1991 and May 1992 as Asian Pacific American Heritage months.

Kristi Yamaguchi

Patricia Saiki, former representative to Congress from Hawaii, was appointed to head the U.S. Small Business Administration by President George Bush.

The Census Bureau reported that the Asian Pacific Islander population in the United States had increased from 3,500,439 in 1980 to 7,273,662 in 1990, a growth of 107.8 percent.

The Japanese American Citizens League Pacific Southwest Regional office in Los Angeles, California, received fifteen hate letters in six months. Phrases like "You birds should move back to Tokyo instead of lobbying constantly for Jap ideas in America" filled the postcards. ("Jap" is a vulgar, derogatory slang term for Japanese.) *(Also see entry dated April 1929.)*

President George Bush appointed Chinese American Elaine Chao to head the Peace Corps. Chao was born in Taiwan and emigrated to the United States with her family in 1961. After receiving her master's degree in business administration from the Harvard Business School and studying at several other distinguished institutions including Columbia University, she pursued a career in international banking and finance. *(Also see entry dated 1989.)*

1992   An economic downturn in the United States inspired a wave of Japan-bashing.

Norman Mineta, representative to the U.S. Congress from San Jose, California, since 1974, was elected chair of the House Public Works and Transportation Committee. *(Also see entry dated November 12, 1932.)*

Korean American Eugene Chung joined the New England Patriots professional football team, becoming the third Asian American, and second Korean American, to play professional football in the United States.

Japanese American Kristi Yamaguchi became the first Asian American to win the Gold Medal for women's figure skating at the 1992 Winter Olympics in Albertville, France. Her career began in 1986 at the Junior Ladies Competition.

Korean American businessman Jay Kim was elected to Congress from the newly created 41st District of California, becoming the first Korean American member of Congress.

Lillian Kimura was elected president of the Japanese American Citizens League. She was the first woman to hold the post. *(Also see entry dated April 1929.)*

Lillian Gonzalez-Pardo, a Filipino American physician, became the first Asian American to be elected national president of the American Medical Women's Association.

Oncologist (physician who is a tumor specialist) Reginald C. S. Ho became the first Native Hawaiian to head the American Cancer Society.

Clayton Fong was appointed deputy assistant to President George Bush in May.

Eugene Huu-Chau Trinh, Vietnamese American physicist, spent fourteen days aboard NASA's first extended-duration space shuttle flight as a payload

Ismail Merchant (left) and James Ivory (right)

specialist (the person in charge of passengers and instruments and other factors related directly to the purpose of the flight).

Chinese American Elaine Chao was selected to head the United Way. *(Also see entry dated 1991.)*

Asian Indian American Ismail Merchant, with collaborator James Ivory, produced a hit film adaptation of E. M. Forster's *Howards End.* *(Also see entry dated 1986.)*

Doug Chiang, born in Taiwan in 1962, won an Academy Award for the creation and design of special effects in the 1992 film *Death Becomes Her*.

An Asian Pacific American Labor Alliance march in Washington, D.C.

May 1. The Asian Pacific American Labor Alliance (APALA), part of the AFL-CIO (American Federation of Labor and Congress of Industrial Organizations), was formed by 500 Asian Pacific American union members with a national office in Washington, D.C., and chapters in various American cities. APALA became a force in the labor movement and a connection for Asian Pacific American workers to the media and the political community.

August 26. Congress passed the Voting Rights Language Assistance Act, which amended the Voting Rights Act of 1965 to require bilingual (dual language) voting materials if more than five percent of the citizens of a state speak a language other than English or are limited in their English proficiency.

1993   Chinese American Connie Chung joined Dan Rather as coanchor of the *CBS Evening News,* a post she held until her firing in 1995. She was also named anchor of a prime-time television news magazine, *Eye to Eye with Connie Chung,* which was cancelled in 1995. *(Also see entry dated August 20, 1946.)*

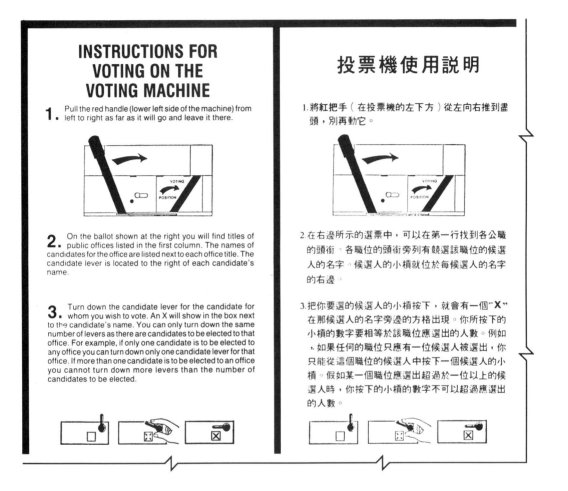

Sample bilingual voting ballot

Maya Lin, Chinese American sculptor and architect, installed *The Women's Table* at Yale University, her alma mater. The granite sculpture and water table (a funnel-shaped hole in the table allows water to seep through) was dedicated to Yale women, past and present. *(Also see entry dated 1981.)*

The Poetry Society of America awarded its prestigious Shelley Memorial Award to Cathy-Lynn Song. Song also won the Hawaii Award for Literature the same year. *(Also see entry dated 1984.)*

Eiko Ishioka, accompanied by presenter Catherine Deneuve, holds her Oscar (Academy Award) for best costume design for *Bram Stoker's Dracula*

Chinese American fashion designer Anna Sui won the Perry Ellis Award for New Fashion Talent.

The film version of author Amy Tan's *The Joy Luck Club* was released to rave reviews. Its success made director Wayne Wang one of the most powerful Asian American directors in Hollywood. *(Also see entry dated 1989.)*

Arati Prabhakar, Asian Indian American scientist, was appointed to head the National Institute of Standards and Technology by President Bill Clinton. She was the first Asian American to hold the post.

Ageless Body, Timeless Mind: The Quantum Alternative to Growing Old, an alternative view of the aging process written by Asian Indian American Deepak Chopra, became an internationally best-selling book.

The coastal freighter *Golden Venture* ran aground in New York Harbor

Samoan American Tiaina (Junior) Seau, Jr., San Diego Chargers linebacker, was named National Football League Player Association Player of the Year by a vote of his peers. He also made his third consecutive trip to the Pro Bowl in four seasons and was named to all-Pro teams by the Associated Press, *Football Digest*, Pro Football Writers Association, *Sporting News*, *College & Pro Football Newsweekly*, and *Sports Illustrated*. Considered one of the finest linebackers in professional football during the 1990s, he would play in the San Diego Chargers' first Super Bowl appearance in 1995.

March 30. Eiko Ishioka won the Academy Award for best costume design for her work in *Bram Stoker's Dracula*.

April 3. Actor Brandon Lee was accidentally shot to death by a prop gun that was thought to be loaded with blanks during the last stages of filming *The Crow*. Lee was the son of Chinese American actor Bruce Lee. *(Also see entry dated November 27, 1940.)*

June 6. The coastal freighter *Golden Venture* ran aground in New York Harbor with 289 Chinese migrants aboard, part of an illegal human smuggling operation. The United States Coast Guard, along with the New York City Fire and Police departments, rescued many from the icy water and evacuated the migrants from the vessel. Eight of the migrants died in their attempt to reach the shore.

July 19. Japanese American Master Sergeant Roy H. Matsumoto, U.S. Army (retired), was inducted into the U.S. Army Ranger Hall of Fame for his extraordinary courage and service with the 5307th Composite Unit (Provisional) during World War II. The unit, better known as Merrill's Marauders, infiltrated Japanese lines and carried out many dangerous missions.

Frederick F. Y. Pang

November 12. Frederick F. Y. Pang, a native of Honolulu, Hawaii, was sworn in as Assistant Secretary of the Navy for Manpower and Reserve Affairs, becoming the highest-ranking Asian American in the U.S. military.

November 23. A joint resolution was passed by Congress to acknowledge the 100th anniversary of the overthrow of the Kingdom of Hawaii and to formally apologize to Native Hawaiians for depriving them of their rights.

Almost thirty years after Hawaii became the 50th state (in 1959), Native Hawaiian activists are working to raise awareness of the negative impact tourism has had on their environment and rich cultural traditions.

1994   Korean American comedian Margaret Cho (born in 1968) was the first Asian American to star in her own television show, *All-American Girl,* a sitcom about a Korean American family.

Native Hawaiian activist march

Chinese American Gus Lee (born 1946) published *Honor and Duty,* the second installment in his semiautobiographical tale of the life of Kai Ting. In *Honor and Duty,* Lee recounts Kai Ting's experiences at West Point (United States Military Academy). *(Also see entry dated 1991.)*

Grandfather's Journey by Allen Say, published in 1993, tells the story of Say's grandfather's life in Japan and America. It won the 1994 Caldecott Medal for most distinguished American children's picture book. (Also see entry dated 1989.)

President Bill Clinton appointed March Fong Eu, then-secretary of state of California, to become ambassador to Micronesia. *(Also see entry dated 1966.)*

Lieutenant Colonel Richard Sakakida, a Japanese American who had worked as a counterintelligence agent in the Philippines during World War II, received the Legion of Honor from the government of the Philippines in recognition of his meritorious service to the Filipino American Freedom Fighters who had sought to oust the Japanese from the Philippines. He was also awarded the Bronze Star by the U.S. Air Force for his distinguished service to the American military.

Actor and director Mako

Asian American environmental activists began to organize advocacy groups in order to educate Asian Americans on the dangers of toxic materials in their environment. One of the key areas of concern was warning labels on toxic materials written only in English and Spanish, leaving many Asian Americans unaware of the danger. Groups such as the Asian Pacific Environmental Network sought to establish ties with mainstream environmental groups to spread information about policies that might adversely affect Asian Americans.

February. Pioneer Asian American actor and director Mako was honored with a star on the Hollywood Walk of Fame. *(Also see entry dated 1965.)*

February 1. Asian Indian American Prema Mathai-Davis became the first foreign-born woman to lead the Young Women's Christian Association (YWCA).

Mathai-Davis was born in the state of Kerala, India. After earning a master's degree in India, she completed a doctorate in human development at Harvard University in 1979. She moved into public service and quickly established herself as a leader in social service programs for the elderly, being appointed New York City's Commissioner in the Department of Aging by Mayor David Dinkins. In 1991 she was appointed to the board of directors of the Metropolitan Transportation Authority of the State of New York.

March. Rajat Gupta became managing director of the major management consulting firm McKinsey and Company. Gupta, born in Calcutta, India, was the first non-Western head of the prestigious company.

March 18. Bruce I. Yamashita, a Japanese American, was commissioned to the rank of captain in the U.S. Marine Corps Reserve after a five-year legal battle to fight the discrimination he had faced in the U.S. Marine Corps Officer Candidate School. He had not been allowed to graduate with his class.

July. Chinese American astronaut Leroy Chiao flew on the space shuttle *Columbia*, conducting life and material science experiments.

Prema Mathai-Davis

July 22. Japanese American Los Angeles superior court judge Lance Ito was assigned to hear the high-profile double-murder case against O. J. Simpson, the Hall of Fame football player and actor who had been accused of murdering his ex-wife and her friend.

September. U.S. Air Force captain Jim Wang, a Chinese American, had court-martial charges brought against him in the friendly-fire (when military personnel are misidentified and accidentally fired on by their own soldiers) deaths of twenty-six Americans aboard two U.S. helicopters flying in a U.S. government-designated "no-fly" zone over Iraq.

Wang was the only one of the six-member crew of the U.S. F-15s who was charged with a crime, the other airmen having had all charges against them dismissed. The Asian American community felt that Wang had become a scapegoat, questioning whether he was singled out as a Chinese American and not just as a lower-ranking officer.

November. Benjamin J. Cayetano (born in 1939) was elected governor of Hawaii, the first Filipino American governor of a state. Cayetano's election as governor made him the highest-ranking elected Filipino American in the United Staes. Prior to his election, he had served as Hawaii's lieutenant governor from 1986 to 1994.

November 8. California voters, by an overwhelming majority, passed Proposition 187, a ballot initiative (nicknamed the "Save our State" initiative) that cut off education and all but emergency health care for undocumented aliens, and required teachers and doctors to report illegal aliens to authorities. Proposition 187 was created to alleviate California's $3 billion per year expenditures on health care and education for the 1.6 million illegal aliens living in the state. The controversial measure was immediately challenged as unconstitutional and looked certain to face years of litigation in the courts.

1995 Eleanor Yu was chosen as the 1995 recipient of the "Entrepreneur of the Year" award by the U. S. Small Business Administration.

She was the first Asian Pacific American, first woman, and the youngest person to receive the award. Yu's Adland Worldwide, a multimillion-dollar advertising agency, boasted several *Fortune* 500 firms as clients, including Coca Cola and MCI Communicatons, Inc.

April 3. Dennis Fung, senior criminalist and eleven-year veteran of the Los Angeles Police Department, began his testimony in the double-murder trial of Hall of Fame football star and media personality O. J. Simpson in Los Angeles. *(Also see entry dated July 22, 1994.)*

May. Connie Chung, co-anchor of the CBS Evening News with Dan Rather, was fired by CBS Broadcast president Peter Lund. Chung claimed that sexism was behind the move and asked to be released from her contract, but other veteran broadcasters believed that sexism was not the issue; in their view, Chung's dismissal was more likely a result of her perceived faults as a hard-news journalist and recent on-air stumbles. *(Also see entry dated August 20, 1946.)*

A. *Magazine*'s February/March issue examined the concerns of the Asian Pacific American community about the "Contract with America" presented by

Eleanor Yu, "Entrepreneur of the Year," 1995

the newly-elected Republican Congress in 1994. The issues highlighted in a special staff editorial were: immigrants and refugees, welfare, affirmative action (an active effort by the government to improve the employment or education opportunities of minority groups and women), health care, education, civil rights, lesbian and gay rights, women's rights, voting and participation of Asian Americans in the political process, communication and the arts, justice and law enforcement, and trade and foreign policy.

FURTHER READING

Asian Americans—General

Asian Americans in the United States, Dubuque, IA: Kendall/Hunt, 1993.

Chan, Sucheng, *Asian Americans: An Interpretive History,* Boston: Twayne Publishers, 1991. Comprehensive history of Asian Americans in the United States. Includes list of films about the Asian American experience, a chronology of Asian American history from 1600 to 1989, and a bibliographic essay describing available works for those interested in further research.

Fawcett, James T., and Benjamin V. Carino, *Pacific Bridges: The New Immigration from Asia and the Pacific Islands,* New York: Center for Migration Studies, 1987.

Furtaw, Julia C., ed., *Asian American Information Directory,* Detroit: Gale Research, 1990.

Hsia, Jayjia, *Asian American in Higher Education and at Work,* Hillsdale, NJ: Lawrence Erlbaum Assoc., Publishers, 1988. A 218-page book reporting on education and employment trends in the 1980s. 83 tables.

Hune, Shirley, *Pacific Migration to the United States: Trends and Themes in Historical and Sociological Literature,* Washington, DC: Research Institute on Immigration and Ethnic Studies, 1977.

Hymns from the Four Winds: A Collection of Asian American Hymns, Nashville, TN: Abingdon Press, 1983.

Kim, Hyung-chan, ed., *Dictionary of Asian American History,* Westport, CT: Greenwood Press, 1986. Entries by various authors on a range of topics.

Kitano, Harry H. L., *Asian Americans: Emerging Minorities,* Englewood Cliffs, NJ: Prentice Hall, 1995. Covers Chinese, Japanese, Korean, Filipino, Asian Indians, Southeast Asians, and Pacific Islanders, with appendix of tables of 1990 U.S. census data, and suggestions for further reading.

Knoll, Tricia, *Becoming Americans: Asian Sojourners, Immigrants, and Refugees in the Western United States,* Portland, OR: Coast to Coast Books, 1982.

Lee, Joann Faung Jean, *Asian American Experiences in the United States: Oral Histories of First to Fourth Generation Americans from China, the Philippines, Japan, India, the Pacific Islands, Vietnam, and Cambodia,* Jefferson, NC: McFarland and Co., 1991.

Mavis, Barbara J., *Contemporary American Success Stories: Famous People of Asian Ancestry,* Childs, MD: Mitchell Lane Publishers, 1994.

Takaki, Ronald, *Spacious Dreams: The First Wave of Asian Immigrants,* New York: Chelsea House, 1994.

Takaki, Ronald, *Strangers from a Different Shore: A History of Asians Americans,* Boston: Little, Brown and Company, 1989. A 570-page book recounting history of Chinese, Japanese, Koreans, Asian Indians, Filipinos, and Southeast Asians, with extensive reference notes and index.

Asian Indian

Chandrasekhar, S., ed., *From India to America,* La Jolla, CA: Population Institute, 1984.

Jensen, Joan M., *Passage from India: Asian Indian Immigrants in North America,* New Haven and London: Yale University Press, 1988. A 350-page book with extensive notes, selected bibliography, and listing of unpublished sources and court cases.

Saran, Parmata, *The Asian Indian Experience in the United States,* Cambridge, MA: Schenkman, 1985.

Chinese

Chan, Sucheng, *This Bittersweet Soil: The Chinese in California Agriculture, 1860-1910,* Berkeley and Los Angeles: University of California Press, 1986.

Chinn, Thomas W., *Bridging the Pacific: San Francisco's Chinatown and Its People,* San Francisco: Chinese Historical Society of America, 1989.

Daniels, Roger, *Asian America: Chinese and Japanese in the U.S. since 1850,* Seattle: University of Washington Press, 1988.

Glick, Clarence E., *Sojourners and Settlers: Chinese Immigrants in Hawaii,* Honolulu: University of Hawaii Press, 1980.

Lyman, Stanford M., *Chinese Americans,* New York: Random House, 1974.

Mark, Diane Mei Lin, *A Place Called Chinese America,* Dubuque, IA: Kendall/Hunt, 1982. A history of Chinese in America prepared under the sponsorship of Organization of Chinese Americans.

Tsai, Shih-san Henry, *The Chinese Experience in America,* Bloomington, IN: Indiana University Press, 1986.

Yung, Judy, *Chinese Women of America: A Pictorial History,* Seattle: University of Washington Press, 1986.

Filipino

Bulosan, Carlos, *America Is in the Heart,* Seattle: University of Washington Press, 1973.

Mangiafico, Luciano, *Contemporary American Immigrants: Patterns of Filipino, Korean,* and Chinese Settlement in the United States, New York: Praeger, 1988.

Teodoro, Luis V., Jr., ed., *Out of This Struggle: The Filipinos in Hawaii,* Honolulu: University of Hawaii Press, 1981.

Japanese

Daniels, Roger, *Concentration Camps, North America: Japanese in the United States and Canada during World War II,* Melbourne, FL: Krieger, 1981.

Houston, Jeanne Wakatsuki, and James D. Houston, *Farewell to Manzanar,* New York: Bantam Books, 1973.

Ichioka, Yuji, *The Issei: The World of the First Generation Japanese Immigrants, 1885-1924,* New York: Free Press, 1989.

Kimura, Yukiko, *Issei: Japanese Immigrants in Hawaii,* Honolulu: University of Hawaii Press, 1988.

Niiya, Brian, ed., *Japanese American History: An A-to-Z Reference from 1868 to the Present,* New York: Facts On File, 1993.

Noda, Kesa, *Yamato Colony, 1906-1960: Livingston, California,* Livingston: Japanese American Citizens League, 1981.

Petersen, William, *Japanese Americans: Oppression and Success,* New York: Random House, 1971.

Korean

Choi, Sook Nyul, *Year of Impossible Goodbyes,* Boston: Houghton Mifflin, 1991.

Choy, Bong-youn, *Koreans in America,* Chicago: Nelson-Hall, 1979.

Yoo, Jay Kun, *The Koreans in Seattle,* Elkins Park, PA: Philip Jaisohn Memorial Foundation, 1979.

Pacific Islanders

Macpherson, Cluny, Bradd Shore, and Robert Franco, eds., *New Neighbors: Islanders in Adaptation,* Santa Cruz, CA: University of California, 1978.

Takaki, Ronald T., *Raising Cane: The World of Plantation Hawaii,* New York: Chelsea House Publishers, 1994.

Vietnamese, Cambodian, Laotian, and Hmong

Criddle, Joan, and Teeda Butt Mam, *To Destroy You Is No Loss: The Odyssey of a Cambodian Family,* New York: Atlantic Monthly Press, 1987.

Espiritu, Yen Le, *Vietnamese in America: An Annotated Bibliography of Materials in Los Angeles and Orange County Libraries,* Los Angeles: Asian American Studies Center, 1988.

Freeman, James A., *Hearts of Sorrow: Vietnamese-American Lives,* Stanford, CA: Stanford University Press, 1989.

Haines, David W., *Refugees as Immigrants: Cambodians, Laotians and Vietnamese in America,* Totowa, NJ: Rowman and Littlefield, 1989.

Hayslip, Le Ly (with Jay Wurts), *When Heaven and Earth Changed Places: A Vietnamese Woman's Journey from War to Peace,* New York: Doubleday, 1989.

Kelly, Gail, *From Vietnam to American: A Chronicle of the Vietnamese Immigrants to the United States,* Boulder, CO: Westview Press, 1978.

Loescher, Gil, and John A. Scanlan, *Calculated Kindness: Refugees and America's Half-Open Door, 1945 to the Present,* New York: Free Press, 1986.

May, Someth, *Cambodian Witness: The Autobiography of Someth May,* New York: Random House, 1986.

Ngor, Haing (with Roger Warner), *Haing Ngor: A Cambodian Odyssey,* New York: MacMillan, 1987.

Szymusial, Molyda, *The Stones Cry Out: A Cambodian Childhood, 1975-1980,* New York: Hill & Wang, 1986.

161

INDEX